30 minute
indian

30 minute
indian

Cook modern
Indian recipes in
30 minutes or under
using ingredients
such as curry leaves,
turmeric, garlic,
saffron, gram flour,
cardamom, ginger,
tamarind, coconut
and chillies.

Sunil Vijayakar
Photography by William Reavell

hamlyn

30 Minute Indian

Sunil Vijayakar

First published in 2000 by Hamlyn, an imprint
of Octopus Publishing Group Limited
2–4 Heron Quays
London E14 4JP

Copyright © 2000 Octopus Publishing Group Limited

ISBN 0 600 600823

Printed in China

Executive Editor:	Polly Manguel
Project Editor:	Cara Frost
Copy-editor:	Linda Doeser
Creative Director:	Keith Martin
Senior Designer:	David Godfrey
Production Controller:	Lisa Moore
Photographer:	William Reavell
Stylist:	Liz Hippisley
Home Economist:	Sunil Vijayakar

Notes

1 Standard level spoon measurements are used in all recipes.
   1 tablespoon = one 15 ml spoon
   1 teaspoon – one 5 ml spoon

2 Imperial and metric measurements have been given in all recipes. Use one set of measurements only and not a mixture of both.

3 Measurements for canned food have been given as a standard metric equivalent.

4 Eggs should be medium unless otherwise stated. The Department of Health advises that eggs should not be consumed raw. This book contains dishes made with raw or lightly cooked eggs. It is prudent for more vulnerable people, such as pregnant and nursing mothers, invalids, the elderly, babies and young children, to avoid uncooked or lightly cooked dishes made with eggs. Once prepared, these dishes should be kept refrigerated and used promptly.

5 Milk should be full fat unless otherwise stated.

6 Fresh herbs should be used unless otherwise stated. If unavailable, use dried herbs as an alternative, but halve the quantities stated.

7 Pepper should be freshly ground black pepper unless otherwise stated.

8 Ovens should be preheated to the specified temperature – if using a fan-assisted oven, follow the manufacturer's instructions for adjusting the time and the temperature.

9 This book includes dishes made with nuts and nut derivatives. It is advisable for customers with known allergic reactions to nuts and nut derivatives and those who may be potentially vulnerable to these allergies, such as pregnant and nursing mothers, invalids, the elderly, babies and children, to avoid dishes made with nuts and nut oils. It is also prudent to check the labels of pre-prepared ingredients for the possible inclusion of nut derivatives.

10 Vegetarians should look for the 'V' symbol on a cheese to ensure that it is made with vegetarian rennet. There are vegetarian forms of Parmesan, feta, Cheddar, Cheshire, Red Leicester, dolcelatte and many goats' cheeses, among others.

contents

introduction

I think my love of food stems from the Sunday mornings I spent with my father as a young boy, growing up in Bombay. A film director with a hectic work and social life, he would make Sunday the day when he would stop and cook a big lunch for a large group of family and friends. He would pile me into his Morris Minor and off we would head for the bustling bazaars and markets. Armed with shopping bags we would wander through endless aisles of vegetable and fruit stalls, then into open courtyards full of fresh fish and shellfish, piled onto blocks of ice, and into tiny little stalls with colourful pyramids of spices, nuts and dried fruits.

This was an experience which assailed all the senses; the visual feast of wicker baskets piled high with bright green bunches of coriander, mint and fenugreek. Wooden crates of mangoes, papayas and ruby-red pomegranates, mountains of fresh ginger, onions and garlic. The tactile experience of touching and tasting the produce, the aromas of all the dried spices and above all, the cacophony of the market sellers plying their wares. Laden with our shopping, we would wend our way home and into the kitchen, where dad would effortlessly conjure up a veritable feast, all the time talking with great passion about different foods and ingredients and making me his official taster. He instilled in me a love and passion for food, with his relaxed attitude to preparation and cooking and most importantly the gift and joy of sharing food.

In this book and through these recipes, I hope I can share with you some of the recipes I have enjoyed and continue to enjoy cooking on a frequent basis. The frenetic pace of our modern life often limits the time we have to spend preparing, cooking and experimenting with food. These recipes are all quick and easy to prepare and will give you a taste of Indian cuisine, which you can easily incorporate into your cooking on a daily basis.

A well-stocked storecupboard of basic ingredients and spices is essential. Most of these can be bought in large supermarkets, but I would urge you to go to an Indian or Asian greengrocer and stock up on a range of ingredients for your storecupboard. All spices, whole or ground, should be stored in airtight containers, in a cool, dark place. Some of the recipes call for a long list of spices and other ingredients; do not let this intimidate you, just make sure that you have everything laid out and at hand before you start to cook and the rest will be easy. You will realize that cooking Indian food is like painting a picture; if you have an organized palette to work with, you can create anything you desire.

The main ingredients for cooking wonderful food are not, however, to be found in spice jars, supermarkets or bazaars, but in the passion, love and joy of cooking, eating and sharing food. Armed with this, you cannot go wrong.

glossary

Amchur
Raw green mango powder, pale yellow in colour. Used in dishes to add tartness with a hint of sweetness. If unavailable, substitute ½ teaspoon of lemon or lime juice for 1 teaspoon of amchur.

Asafoetida
A resin from the plant, it is extremely strong in flavour and aroma and is used only in tiny quantities. It is available in small plastic boxes and should be stored tightly closed. As well as flavour, asafoetida has great digestive powers.

Atta or Chapatti Flour
This medium-grade flour is used to make most Indian unleavened breads. This may be bought at any Indian grocers. Ordinary wholemeal flour may also be used for Indian breads, very well sieved.

Basmati Rice
This distinctive long grain rice is very popular as an accompaniment to meat and vegetable dishes.

Cardamom
Little green pods with tiny black-brown seeds, very aromatic in flavour. They come in three varieties: green, white and black. The green and white pods can be used for both sweet and savoury dishes or to flavour rice, the black only for savoury dishes. The pods are used whole in rice dishes or the seeds are lightly crushed or ground and used to flavour sweets and other dishes. It is one of the main components of garam masala.

Cashew Nuts
Grown on the western coast of India, these nuts are used in curries, rice dishes and desserts. They are usually roasted or fried before being used.

Cassia
Also known as 'Chinese cinnamon', this bark is stronger in flavour than cinnamon and has a slightly thicker texture. It can easily be substituted with cinnamon, if unavailable.

Chillies, dried
These red chillies are used to flavour dishes, usually by frying them in hot oil. There are a few varieties such as the Kashmiri and Round chillies. Chilli flakes are also used in cooking to give a fiery 'heat' to food. Use with caution.

Chillies, fresh green and red
The chillies used in Indian food are usually the long green, slender variety and can be very hot in flavour. To lessen the heat of a chilli, when using, carefully remove the seeds by splitting the chilli in half lengthways, using gloves if need be. Fresh red chillies are simply ripened green chillies and have the same intensity of heat.

Chilli Powder
Mild, medium and hot chilli powders are made from powdered dried chillies. If using for the first time, experiment with the amount that you use.

Cinnamon
Cinnamon is the thinly rolled inner bark of an evergreen tree that grows mainly in southern India and Sri Lanka, in Madagascar and in the West Indies.Used in stick or powdered form, this bark is used to flavour rice dishes, curries and sweets. It can be substituted with cassia bark if the recipe calls for it.

Cloves
This very strongly-flavoured and aromatic spice is used in many curry and rice dishes. Ground or powdered cloves are used in very small quantities because of their pungency. It is also sometimes used to seal a betel leaf for serving after an Indian meal.

Coconut
Fresh coconut flesh is widely used in many Indian dishes, grated or ground to a paste. To obtain the flesh from a coconut, the easiest way I have found is to put it into a thick plastic bag and slam it hard on a concrete floor. There will be some water in it which you can save and then you should prise the flesh from the tough outer shell with a sharp knife. Once this is done, remove the thin brown skin, using a vegetable peeler. To get grated coconut for a recipe, cut the flesh into small pieces and process in a food processor or blender, until you get tiny flakes. You can also use a conventional grater, which is time consuming, but you will get a smoother texture. Grated coconut freezes well if stored in an airtight freezer bag and is always useful to have on hand.

Coconut Milk
Providing texture and flavour to meat and vegetable dishes, this milk is widely available in supermarkets and is sold in 400 g (13 oz) cans.

Coriander, dried
This spice is sold as whole seeds, which are light brown and round, or

as a ground powder. It is an essential spice in Indian cooking.

Coriander, fresh
This fragrant and aromatic herb is widely used in Indian cuisine and is an important ingredient for many dishes, chutneys and salads.

Cumin
These little brown grain-like seeds are used whole, fried or roasted, in Indian dishes. In its ground form, cumin is an essential base to many dishes, from curries to rice.

Curry Leaves
These leaves are small and dark green and are often sold fresh in Indian greengrocers. They are usually fried before use, to impart an aromatic flavour to any dish or pickle.

Dhal
These are pulses and lentils and there are over sixty different types. The better known are listed below, and are available in Indian grocery stores and large supermarkets.
Masoor dhal are split, skinless, red lentils. They are dark brown when whole but when split and the skin is removed , the colour is bright pinky orange.
Moong dhal are split, skinless, moong lentils. They are dark green when whole but once split and skinned they are yellow and oval shaped.
Channa dhal are split, black, gram lentils, They are from the chick-pea family but are smaller and have a dark brown husk. When split and skinned they are bright yellow and resemble yellow split peas. Gram flour (besan) is made from these lentils.

Dhana-jeera
A mixture of powdered coriander and cumin seeds, sold in Asian greengrocers. You can make your own mix by grinding together 1 teaspoon of cumin seeds and 2 teaspoons coriander seeds.

Fennel Seeds
These light green seeds have a flavour of anise and are slightly bigger than cumin seeds. They are also eaten, lightly roasted, after an Indian meal as a digestive.

Fenugreek Seeds and Leaves
These tiny, pebble-like, mustard-yellow seeds have an earthy flavour and are mainly used in pickles and vegetarian cooking. When the seeds are sprouted, it results in a spinach-like leaf, which is used to flavour breads and other dishes.

Garam Masala
This is a ground spice mix, used to flavour food. It can be bought in ready-made commercial jars or packets. However, there is nothing like making your own, as it will have much more pungency and flavour. The main ingredients of are cardamom, cinnamon or cassia bark, cloves and black peppercorns. Here is a recipe for making you own. Once made, store in an airtight jar and use when required.

1 tablespoon cassia or cinnamon
  sticks, broken up
1 tablespoon cardamom pods
1 teaspoon whole cloves
3 teaspoons cumin seeds
2 teaspoons black peppercorns

In a dry, hot frying pan, roast the spices for 1–2 minutes, or until you can smell the aroma. Cool and place in a coffee grinder and blend until you have a fine powder. Store in an airtight jar. This mixture will keep for 3–4 months.

Garlic
Indispensable to most Indian cooking, fresh garlic is used peeled and finely crushed, chopped or sliced. A quick way to get crushed garlic is to use a fine grater.

Ginger
This rhizome is an integral part of most Indian cooking, along with garlic and onions (the essential base of most Indian food). Make sure you get fresh ginger which has a smooth light brown skin. To use, peel and either slice into slivers or fine dice, or finely grate, saving and using any juice.

Gram Flour
A fine, pale yellow coloured flour made from chickpeas. It is used in many recipes from breads to vegetable curries.

Green Mangoes
The unripe fruit with green skin is used mainly as a pickle ingredient and sometimes to add a tangy flavour to curries.

Jaggery
Raw cane sugar, sold in blocks or moulds and widely used to sweeten or balance any hot, spicy dish. However, if not available, soft brown cane sugar can easily replace it.

Mango Pulp
A versatile ingredient, usually used to flavour drinks.

glossary

Mustard Seeds
Brown and black mustard seeds are used as an essential part of flavouring in Indian cooking. They are usually fried quickly in hot oil until they start to pop and they flavour many pickles, vegetarian dishes, dhals and rice dishes. They have a wonderfully nutty flavour when cooked.

Nigella
Also known as black onion seeds, these tiny tear-drop seeds are very aromatic when cooked and are used to flavour breads and pickles.

Nutmeg
Nutmeg is the seed of the nutmeg tree. It grows within a lacy cage of mace, inside a fleshy peach-like fruit. It is dried in the sun after havesting, and is sold both whole and in pow-dered form. Although very hard to grate, the whole nutmeg may be cracked easily with a hammer. It is best bought whole as the ground form soon loses its fragrance.

Okra
Known as bhindi in India, okra are the seed pods of a member of the hibiscus family. Choose bright green, firm specimens with no signs of browning

Onion Seeds
Black in colour and triangular in shape, these are used for both pickles and vegetable curries.

Paan
Betel leaf dressed with calcium paste, fennel seeds wrapped and held together with a clove and sometimes covered with varq, for serving at the end of the evening to guests at an Indian party. It acts as a mouth-freshener and coats the mouth with a red colouring.

Poppy seeds
These dried whole seeds are always better when toasted. They are used, often whole, to flavour curries. Although they are from the opium poppy, they do not contain opium.

Raita
A cool dip consisting of yoghurt with either onions or cumber is often served as an accompaniment to hot, spicy dishes.

Rose Water
The essence of roses which is used mainly to flavour Indian sweet dishes. Rose petals are widely used to garnish food as well.

Saffron
This highly valued and expensive spice consists of dried stigma's from a special crocus. Used to flavour rice and sweets, it is only used in very small quantities. Saffron is sold both as strands and in powder form. It has a beautiful flavour and fragrance.

Seasame seeds
Whole, flat, cream-coloured seeds, these are used to flavour some curries. When ground they can be made into chutney.

Shallots
The shallot is widely used in Indian cooking along with onions and spring onions. The shallot is suited to the making of flavourings of sauces because of its subtlety of flavour and the way in which its tender flesh cooks to such softness.

Tamarind
This is a pod-like fruit from a tall, shade tree and the dried, or semi-dried pulp is used for cooking. It is usually sold in blocks and to obtain a purée or paste to use in cooking, it has to be soaked in hot water for a couple of hours, then the pulp can be sieved for use. It gives food a sour and slightly sweet flavour. However, commercially produced tamarind paste is widely available now.

Tandoori Masala
A commercially produced Indian spice powder mix which livens up any curry. It can also be used as part of amarinade mixture.

Turmeric
A rhizome, which when dried, results in a bright yellow powder. This musky spice is used in small quantities mainly in vegetable and lentil dishes.

Varq
Edible beaten silver leaf used for decoration purposes. It should be handled gently as it is very light and airy. It can be bought in sheets from Indian or Pakistani grocers.

soups,
starters
& snacks

Most of these dishes are
usually served as part of
a main Indian meal. Here
however, they make easy
and elegant starters and
snacks. Alternatively, serve
with salad and bread for
a wonderfully light meal.

Preparation time 10 minutes Cooking time 20 minutes Total time 30 minutes Serves 4

khandvi

4 tablespoons gram flour (besan)
1 tablespoon natural yogurt
2 teaspoons sea salt
¼ teaspoon ground turmeric
¼ teaspoon asafoetida
1 teaspoon chilli powder
500 ml/17 fl oz water
2 tablespoons sunflower oil
8–10 curry leaves
2 teaspoons mustard seeds
1 tablespoon grated fresh coconut
1 tablespoon chopped fresh coriander leaves

These lightly spiced rolls are the Indian equivalent of pasta, but are made from gram flour (besan). Flavoured with coconut, coriander and mustard seeds, they make a wonderful cold starter.

one In a bowl, whisk together the flour, yogurt, salt, turmeric, asafoetida, chilli powder and water.

two Put this mixture in a heavy-based saucepan and bring to the boil, stirring occasionally.

three Lower the heat and cook, stirring frequently, for 10–15 minutes until thick. Remove from the heat.

four Lightly oil a 30 x 30 cm/12 x 12 inch baking sheet and spoon the mixture on to the tray, spreading it thinly over the surface with the back of a wide spoon. Leave for about 5-10 minutes to cool, then cut into 2.5 cm/1 inch strips and roll up into mini Swiss rolls. Divide between 4 plates and set aside.

five Heat the oil in a small saucepan and, when hot, add the curry leaves and mustard seeds. As soon as the seeds start to pop, spoon the oil over the rolls. Sprinkle over the coconut and coriander and serve.

Preparation time 5 minutes Cooking time 15 minutes Total time 20 minutes Serves 4

paneer tikka

1 tablespoon sunflower oil
15 g/½ oz butter
1 teaspoon cumin seeds
200 g/7 oz chestnut mushrooms, thinly sliced
250 g/8 oz paneer, cut into bite-sized cubes
1 teaspoon sea salt
1 teaspoon freshly ground black pepper
1 teaspoon tandoori masala powder
a handful of chopped coriander
1 tablespoon lemon juice
shredded iceberg lettuce
mint leaves, to garnish

Ready-prepared paneer is now widely available and can be found in the cheese section of many supermarkets. However, it is simple to make your own (see page 34).

one Heat the oil and butter in a large wok or nonstick frying pan and when hot, add the cumin and mushrooms. Fry, stirring, for 5–7 minutes.

two Add the paneer, salt, pepper, tandoori masala, coriander and lemon juice and cook over a low heat, stirring occasionally, for 7–8 minutes.

three To serve, arrange some shredded lettuce on each plate and top with the paneer tikka. Garnish with mint leaves and serve warm.

Preparation time 10 minutes Cooking time 20 minutes Total time 30 minutes Makes 6 pancakes

spiced spinach and carrot pancakes

75 g/3 oz carrots, grated
75 g/3 oz spinach, roughly chopped
1 onion, finely chopped
2 fresh green chillies, deseeded and chopped
1 teaspoon fennel seeds
1 tablespoon ground coriander
100 g/3½ oz gram flour (besan), sieved
50 g/2 oz semolina
1 teaspoon baking powder
300 ml/½ pint water
vegetable oil
sea salt

These pancakes from Gujerat are made from gram flour (besan) and are known as 'pudlas'. Serve them as a starter, with Cucumber and Pomegranate Raita (see page 27).

one In a large bowl mix together the carrots, spinach, onion, chillies, fennel seeds and coriander. Season with salt and set aside.

two Mix together the gram flour, semolina and baking powder and add to the carrot mixture.

three Add the water gradually to the mixture, mixing well with a spoon, until you have a thick batter.

four Lightly grease a nonstick frying pan with oil. When hot, add 2 tablespoons of the mixture and spread with a spatula to make a pancake about 17–18 cm/6½–7 inches in diameter. Cover and cook for 1–2 minutes, or until the pancake is lightly browned on the base, then flip over and cook for another 2 minutes. Repeat with the remaining batter to make 6 pancakes. Serve them hot.

Tip: The cooked pancakes can be stored on a lined baking sheet, stacked and interleaved with greaseproof paper, and kept in a low oven 110°C (225°F), Gas Mark ¼, until you are ready to serve them.

Preparation time 10 minutes, plus resting

Cooking time 10 minutes Total time 20 minutes Makes 10-12

onion bhajiyas

1 onion, halved and thinly sliced
5 tablespoons gram flour (besan)
1 tablespoon sunflower oil
2 teaspoons sea salt
1 teaspoon sugar
1 teaspoon lemon juice
1 teaspoon ground cumin
1 fresh green chilli, deseeded and finely chopped
1 tablespoon chopped fresh coriander
¾ teaspoon baking powder
2-3 tablespoons water
vegetable oil, for deep-frying

A popular snack sold on almost every street corner in India, these bhajiyas are delicious served hot with Tamarind and Date Chutney (see page 30) and Coconut Chutney (see page 37).

one Mix all the ingredients together in a bowl (apart from the oil for deep-frying) and let the mixture rest for 10 minutes.

two Using your hands, mix well to combine thoroughly.

three Heat the oil in a wok to 180–190°C (350–375°F), or until a cube of bread browns in 30 seconds, and then drop spoonfuls of the mixture into the oil and deep-fry for 1–2 minutes, until golden. You might have to do this in 2-3 batches.

four Serve hot with tamarind and date chutney and/or coconut chutney.

Preparation time 10 minutes, plus marinating

Cooking time 4–5 minutes Total time 15 minutes Serves 4

prawn and mango kebabs

16 large raw tiger prawns, peeled and deveined
1 tablespoon sunflower oil
4 tablespoons lemon juice
2 garlic cloves, crushed
1 teaspoon grated fresh root ginger
1 teaspoon chilli powder
1 tablespoon clear honey
1 teaspoon sea salt
1 large mango, peeled, stoned and cut into 8 bite-sized pieces
dressed salad, to serve

These kebabs make a colourful and elegant starter.

one Put the prawns in a large bowl and add the oil, lemon juice, garlic, ginger, chilli powder, honey and salt. Mix well and marinate for about 10 minutes.

two Remove the prawns from the marinade and thread 2 prawns alternately between 2 pieces of mango on each of 8 skewers.

three Place the skewers under a preheated hot grill, brush with the remaining marinade and grill for 2 minutes on each side, or until the prawns turn pink and are cooked through.

four Serve 2 skewers on each plate, with some dressed salad.

Preparation time 10 minutes Cooking time 20 minutes Total time 30 minutes Serves 4

coriander chicken kebabs

a handful of roughly chopped fresh coriander
2 tablespoons chopped mint leaves
5 garlic cloves, roughly chopped
2 teaspoons grated fresh root ginger
1 teaspoon ground cumin
1 teaspoon ground coriander
1 fresh green chilli, roughly chopped
2 teaspoons soft brown sugar
400 g/13 oz minced chicken
100 g/3½ oz fresh breadcrumbs
sea salt and pepper
lemon wedges, to serve

Serve these delicious kebabs on their own as a starter or with salad for a light lunch.

one Put the chopped coriander, mint, garlic, ginger, cumin, ground coriander, chilli and sugar in a food processor and process until fairly smooth. Season with salt and pepper.

two Turn the mixture into a large bowl and add the chicken and breadcrumbs. Mix well, using your hands.

three Divide the mixture into 12 and shape around metal or presoaked wooden skewers, using your hands.

four Arrange the kebabs on a wire rack on a baking sheet and bake in a preheated oven, 200°C (400°F), Gas Mark 6, for 20 minutes.

five Serve hot, with lemon wedges.

Preparation time 15 minutes Cooking time 15 minutes Total time 30 minutes Makes 20

spicy fish cakes

425 g/14 oz cooked cod fillet
2 potatoes, boiled and mashed
4 spring onions, thinly sliced
2 fresh green chillies, deseeded and finely chopped
1 teaspoon grated fresh root ginger
2 garlic cloves, crushed
4 tablespoons chopped fresh coriander leaves
2 eggs
fresh breadcrumbs, for coating
vegetable oil
sea salt and pepper

Salmon could easily replace the cod in these delicious fish cakes. Serve them with the Kachumber (see page 37) and Mango, Apple and Mint Chutney (see page 35).

one Flake the fish into a bowl and add the potatoes, spring onions, chillies, ginger, garlic and coriander. Season with salt and pepper and add 1 egg. Mix well.

two Shape the fish mixture into 20 small cakes and set aside.

three Beat the remaining egg in a shallow bowl, dip the cakes in the egg and then coat with the breadcrumbs.

four Heat the oil in a large nonstick frying pan and fry the cakes, in batches, for 2 minutes on each side, or until golden brown. Serve hot.

akuri

15 g/½ oz butter
1 small red onion, finely chopped
1 fresh green chilli, finely sliced
8 organic eggs, lightly beaten
1 tablespoon crème fraîche
1 tomato, finely chopped
1 tablespoon chopped fresh coriander leaves
sea salt
buttered toast, to serve

These spicy scrambled eggs make a wonderful 'pick-me-up' breakfast or an equally good starter, served with hot buttered toast or toasted ciabatta.

one Heat the butter in a large nonstick frying pan and add the onion and chilli. Stir-fry for 1–2 minutes.

two Add the eggs, crème fraîche, tomato and coriander. Season with salt and cook over a medium-low heat, stirring frequently, for about 3–4 minutes, or until the eggs are lightly scrambled and set. Serve hot with buttered toast.

tomato and coriander soup

2 tablespoons sunflower oil
4 spring onions
4 curry leaves or 1 bay leaf
400 g/13 oz can chopped tomatoes
1 teaspoon sea salt
1 garlic clove, crushed
1 teaspoon black peppercorns, roughly crushed
3 tablespoons chopped fresh coriander leaves
500 ml/17 fl oz vegetable stock
200 ml/7 fl oz single cream
hot crusty bread, to serve

Use homemade or good quality vegetable stock to make this flavoursome soup.

one Heat the oil in a large saucepan and, when hot, add the spring onions, curry leaves or bay leaf and tomatoes and cook over a medium heat for 2–3 minutes.

two Add the salt, garlic, peppercorns, coriander and vegetable stock. Stir and bring to the boil. Cover the pan, lower the heat and simmer gently for 10 minutes.

three Stir in the cream and cook gently for 1–2 minutes.

four Ladle the soup into 4 bowls and serve with hot crusty bread.

Preparation time 10 minutes **Cooking time** 15-20 minutes **Total time** 25-30 minutes **Makes** 12

vegetable samosas

3 large potatoes, boiled and roughly mashed
100 g/3½ oz cooked peas
1 teaspoon cumin seeds
1 teaspoon amchur (dried mango powder)
2 fresh green chillies, deseeded and finely chopped
1 small red onion, finely chopped
3 tablespoons chopped fresh coriander leaves
1 tablespoon chopped mint leaves
4 tablespoons lemon juice
12 filo pastry sheets, each about 30 x 18 cm/12 x 7 inches
melted butter, for brushing
sea salt and pepper

These crisp savouries can be made in advance and frozen. They can then be cooked straight from the freezer. Serve with Coconut Chutney (see page 37).

one In a large bowl, mix together the potatoes, peas, cumin, amchur, chillies, onion, coriander, mint and lemon juice. Season with salt and pepper to taste and set aside.

two Fold each sheet of filo pastry in half lengthways. Put a large spoonful of the potato mixture at one end and then fold the corner of the pastry over the mixture, covering it in a triangular shape. Continue folding over the triangle of pastry along the length of the pastry strip to make a neat triangular samosa.

three Place the samosas on a baking sheet lined with nonstick baking paper, brush with melted butter and bake in a preheated oven, 200°C (400°F), Gas Mark 6, for 15–20 minutes, or until golden.

salads &
side dishes

These accompaniments of
salads, relishes, pickles and
chutneys form an integral
part of any Indian meal.

Preparation time 10 minutes Total time 10 minutes Serves 4

chickpea salad

400 g/13 oz can chickpeas, rinsed and drained
½ iceberg lettuce, finely shredded
1 cucumber, finely diced
1 small red onion, halved and thinly sliced
4 plum tomatoes, roughly chopped
fresh coriander leaves, to garnish
For the dressing:
1 garlic clove, crushed
1 tablespoon olive oil
2 tablespoons lime juice
1 teaspoon caster sugar
½ teaspoon ground cumin
½ teaspoon ground coriander

A mildly spiced dressing adds a kick to this nutritious salad.

one Put the chickpeas, lettuce, cucumber, onion and tomatoes in a wide, shallow serving dish or bowl.

two Mix together the ingredients for the dressing and pour over the salad.

three Toss to mix well and serve garnished with coriander leaves.

potato and red kidney bean salad

400 g/13 oz potatoes, peeled and cut into
2.5 cm/1 inch cubes
250 ml/8 fl oz Greek yogurt
1 garlic clove, crushed
1 fresh red chilli, thinly sliced
1 teaspoon clear honey
2 tablespoons lime juice
4 tablespoons chopped dill
4 spring onions, thinly sliced
400 g/13 oz canned red kidney beans, drained
and rinsed
sea salt and pepper

This substantial salad is a superb variation on a traditional dish.

one Boil the potatoes in a large pan of water until tender. Drain and set aside.

two In a bowl, mix together the yogurt, garlic, chilli, honey, lime juice and dill. Set aside.

three Transfer the potatoes to a salad bowl and add the spring onions and red kidney beans. Pour over the yogurt and dill mixture, season with salt and pepper and serve at room temperature.

cucumber and pomegranate raita

250 ml/8 fl oz natural yogurt
1 cucumber, peeled, deseeded and finely
chopped
2 tablespoons chopped mint leaves
1 tablespoon chopped fresh coriander
seeds from ½ pomegranate
sea salt and pepper

This bejewelled raita is the perfect foil to any hot and spicy dish.

one Beat the yogurt in a bowl and add the cucumber, mint, coriander and pomegranate seeds. Season with salt and pepper and chill until ready to serve.

Preparation time 10 minutes Cooking time 8–10 minutes Total time 18–20 minutes Serves 4

lobia salad

2 potatoes, cut into small cubes
100 g/3½ oz green beans, cut into
2.5 cm/1 inch pieces
400 g/13 oz can black-eyed beans, rinsed and drained
4 spring onions, thinly sliced
1 fresh green chilli, deseeded and finely chopped
1 tomato, roughly chopped
a handful of mint leaves
hot, toasted Naan (see page 103), to serve
For the dressing:
2 tablespoons light olive oil
1 tablespoon lemon juice
½ teaspoon chilli powder
1 teaspoon clear honey
sea salt and pepper

Black-eyed beans feature in this unusual salad.

one Cook the potatoes and green beans in a large pan of boiling water for 8–10 minutes. Drain and place in a large serving bowl.

two Add the black-eyed beans, spring onions, chilli, tomato and mint leaves. Toss to mix well.

three Combine all the dressing ingredients in a small bowl and mix well. Pour over the salad, mix well and serve with hot toasted naan bread.

Preparation time 10 minutes Total time 10 minutes Makes about 200 g/7 oz

tamarind and date chutney

200 g/7 oz pitted dried dates, roughly chopped
1 tablespoon tamarind paste
1 teaspoon ground cumin
1 teaspoon chilli powder
1 tablespoon tomato ketchup
200 ml/7 fl oz water
sea salt

This sweet and sour relish makes a great accompaniment to any Indian meal, but it is wonderful in a cheese sandwich as well.

one Put all the ingredients in a food processor or blender and process until fairly smooth.

two Transfer to a serving bowl, cover and chill until required. It will keep for up to 3 days in the refrigerator.

Preparation time 5 minutes Total time 5 minutes Makes 8–10

lasan chutney

12 garlic cloves, chopped
1 teaspoon chilli powder
2 fresh red chillies, chopped
1 tablespoon vegetable oil
1 teaspoon sea salt
1 tablespoon lime juice

This spicy accompaniment is not for the faint hearted. It is wonderful with rice dishes and can really spice up a sandwich.

one Put all the ingredients in a food processor or blender and process until smooth. Alternatively, pound to a paste in a mortar with a pestle. This chutney will keep well for up to 2 weeks, stored in an airtight container in the refrigerator.

Preparation time 10 minutes Cooking time 7–8 minutes Total time 17–18 minutes Serves 4

cauliflower relish

2 tablespoons vegetable oil
2 teaspoons black mustard seeds
½ teaspoon ground turmeric
½ teaspoon asafoetida
1 small cauliflower, cut into bite-sized pieces
1 red onion, finely chopped
1 fresh green chilli, deseeded and finely chopped
lemon juice
sea salt

This is delicious as an accompaniment to kebabs and samosas.

one Heat the oil in a large nonstick frying pan and, when hot, add the mustard seeds, turmeric and asafoetida. When the seeds start to pop, add the cauliflower, onion and chilli. Stir-fry for 5 minutes and then remove from the heat. The cauliflower should have a bite to it.

two Season with lemon juice and salt to taste. Serve at room temperature.

Preparation time 10 minutes Cooking time 2–3 minutes Total time 12–13 minutes Serves 4

ginger relish

2 tablespoons grated fresh root ginger
2 garlic cloves, roughly chopped
1 tablespoon grated fresh coconut or
2 tablespoons desiccated coconut
2 fresh green chillies, deseeded
1 teaspoon sea salt
1 teaspoon sugar
150 ml/¼ pint natural yogurt, beaten
2 tablespoons vegetable oil
1 teaspoon black mustard seeds
6-8 curry leaves

This southern Indian relish is a delicious accompaniment to any meal.

one Put the ginger, garlic, coconut, chillies, salt and sugar in a food processor or blender and process until smooth. Add the yogurt and process for a few seconds.

two Transfer to a bowl and set aside.

three Heat the oil in a small frying pan and add the mustard seeds and curry leaves. When the mustard seeds start to pop, remove the pan from the heat and pour the spiced oil over the yogurt mixture. Mix well and chill until required.

Preparation time 10 minutes Cooking time 2–3 minutes Total time 12–13 minutes Serves 4

gujarati carrot salad

500 g/1 lb carrots, coarsely grated
4 tapblespoons lemon juice
1 tablespoon clear honey
1 tablespoon vegetable oil
½ teaspoon dried chilli flakes
2 teaspoons black mustard seeds
4 curry leaves
sea salt

Hot spicy oil and honey create a delicious sweet-and-sour dressing for this simple salad.

one Place the carrots in a serving bowl.

two Mix together the lemon juice and honey and pour over the carrots. Season with salt.

three Heat the oil in a small saucepan and, when hot, add the chilli flakes, mustard seeds and curry leaves. As soon as the mustard seeds start to pop, remove the pan from the heat and pour the dressing over the carrots. Stir well to mix.

Preparation time 2 minutes **Cooking time** 15–20 minutes, plus setting

Total time 14 minutes **Makes** about 150 g/5 oz

paneer

1 litre/1¾ pints full fat milk
2 tablespoons lemon juice

This fresh cheese is now widely available from supermarkets, but it is really special and satisfying when made from scratch. Use in the recipe for Paneer Tikka (see page 14) or serve it on hot Naan (see page 103) with a relish or pickle.

one Heat the milk in a large saucepan and bring to the boil.

two Add the lemon juice, stirring continuously, until the milk thickens and then begins to curdle.

three Strain the curdled milk through a fine sieve, discarding the whey.

four Turn the cheese out on to a clean chopping board and sandwich with another clean board. Put a heavy weight on top and leave to set for 1 hour. Once set, the cheese can be cut or crumbled into other dishes.

Preparation time 10 minutes Cooking time 5 minutes, plus maturing

Total time 15 minutes Makes 1 jar

lime pickle

10 limes, each cut into 6 sections
100 g/3½ oz sea salt
1 tablespoon fenugreek seeds
1 tablespoon black mustard seeds
1 tablespoon chilli powder
1 tablespoon ground turmeric
300 ml/½ pint vegetable oil
½ teaspoon ground asafoetida

This pickle is a wonderful accompaniment to rice, yogurt and a simple dhal.

one Place the limes in a sterilized jar and cover with the salt.

two In a small frying pan, dry-fry the fenugreek and mustard seeds and then grind them to a powder.

three Add the ground seeds, chilli powder and turmeric to the limes and mix well.

four Heat the oil in a small frying pan until smoking, add the asafoetida and fry for 30 seconds. Pour the oil over the limes and mix well.

five Cover the jar with a clean cloth and leave to mature for 10 days in a bright, warm place. Store the pickle in a tightly covered container. This pickle can be kept for a couple of months.

Tip: Grind the spices in a mortar with a pestle, a spice grinder or a coffee grinder kept specially for the purpose.

Preparation time 10 minutes Total time 10 minutes Serves 4–6

mango, apple and mint chutney

1 raw green mango, peeled stoned and roughly chopped
1 small apple, peeled, cored and roughly chopped
1 teaspoon sea salt
1 tablespoon chopped mint leaves
1 teaspoon mild chilli powder
1 teaspoon soft brown sugar
150 ml/¼ pint water

This relish is a tasty accompaniment to many snacks. Try it with Spicy Fish Cakes (see page 20).

one Put all the ingredients in a food processor or blender and process until smooth.

two Transfer to a small serving dish, cover and store in the refrigerator until required.

Preparation time 10 minutes Total time 10 minutes Makes about 250 g/8 oz

coriander chutney

250 g/8 oz chopped fresh coriander leaves
and stalks
4 fresh green chillies, deseeded
2 teaspoons grated fresh root ginger
4 garlic cloves, chopped
2 teaspoons caster sugar
1 teaspoon ground cumin
4 tablespoons lemon juice
3 tablespoons chopped mint leaves
200 ml/7 fl oz water
sea salt

This vibrant green chutney is wonderful spread into cucumber sandwiches, adds zing when used as a marinade for grilled fish and livens up any soup or dhal.

one Put all the ingredients in a food processor or blender and process until smooth.

two Transfer the chutney to a serving bowl and keep covered in the refrigerator until ready to use. It will keep for up to 3–4 days in the refrigerator.

Preparation time 10 minutes Cooking time 2–3 minutes Total time 12–13 minutes Serves 4

coconut chutney

100 g/3½ oz grated fresh coconut
3 fresh green chillies, deseeded
1 teaspoon sugar
2 teaspoons grated fresh root ginger
150 ml/¼ pint natural yogurt
2 tablespoons vegetable oil
2 teaspoons black mustard seeds
6–8 curry leaves
sea salt

This chutney is a terrific accompaniment to Vegetable Samosas (see page 22).

one Put the coconut, chillies, sugar, ginger and yogurt in a food processor or blender and process until smooth. Transfer to a bowl and set aside.

two Heat the oil in a small frying pan and, when hot, add the mustard seeds and curry leaves. As soon as the seeds start to pop, remove the pan from the heat and pour the spicy oil over the yogurt mixture. Season with salt to taste. Chill until ready to serve.

Preparation time 10 minutes, plus resting Total time 10 minutes Serves 4

kachumber

1 red onion, halved and thinly sliced
2 ripe plum tomatoes, finely chopped
1 small cucumber, peeled and finely chopped
1 fresh green chilli, deseeded and thinly sliced
a handful of chopped fresh coriander leaves
4 tablespoons lemon juice
½ teaspoon sugar
sea salt and pepper

Tomatoes, onion and cucumber feature in this traditional and refreshing salad.

one Mix all the ingredients in a bowl, season with salt and pepper and allow to rest for at least 15 minutes before serving.

meat & poultry

Yogurt is used widely
in India for marinating
meat and poultry. The
yogurt tenderizes the
meat and gives a silken
texture and wonderful
flavour when coupled
with other spices
and herbs.

Preparation time 10 minutes, plus marinating (optional)

Cooking time 20 minutes Total time 30 minutes Serves 4

tandoori chicken

4 large chicken quarters, skinned
200 ml/7 fl oz natural yogurt
1 teaspoon grated fresh root ginger
2 garlic cloves, crushed
1 teaspoon garam masala
2 teaspoons ground coriander
¼ teaspoon ground turmeric
1 tablespoon tandoori masala
4 tablespoons lemon juice
1 tablespoon vegetable oil
sea salt
lime or lemon wedges, to garnish

The flavour of this chicken dish when cooked in a tandoor (clay oven) is sublime. However, this recipe comes very close to capturing the real thing.

one Place the chicken in a non-metallic, shallow, ovenproof dish and make 3 deep slashes in each piece, to allow the flavours to penetrate. Set aside.

two Mix together the yogurt, ginger, garlic, garam masala, ground coriander, turmeric, tandoori masala, lemon juice and oil. Season with salt and spread over the chicken pieces to cover. Cover and marinate overnight in the refrigerator, if time allows.

three Bake the chicken in a preheated oven, 240°C (475°F), Gas Mark 9, for 20 minutes, or until cooked through. Remove from the oven and serve hot, garnished with lime or lemon wedges.

Preparation time 10 minutes   Cooking time 15 minutes   Total time 25 minutes   Serves 4

ginger chicken

250 ml/8 fl oz natural yogurt
1 tablespoon grated fresh root ginger
2 garlic cloves, crushed
1 tablespoon chilli powder
1 tablespoon ground coriander
2 teaspoons ground cumin
2 tablespoons vegetable oil
250 g/8 oz chicken thighs, skinned, boned and cut into bite-sized pieces
150 ml/¼ pint chicken stock
sea salt and pepper
chopped fresh coriander, to garnish

one In a bowl, mix together the yogurt, ginger, garlic, chilli powder, ground coriander and cumin. Season with salt and pepper.

two Heat the oil in a large nonstick frying pan and, when hot, add the chicken. Stir-fry for 4–5 minutes, or until sealed.

three Add the yogurt mixture and the stock. Bring to the boil, cover and cook gently for 8–10 minutes, stirring frequently, until the chicken is tender and cooked through. Serve hot, garnished with chopped coriander

chettinad chicken

2 tablespoons sunflower oil
1 onion, halved and thinly sliced
10 curry leaves
1 fresh green chilli, chopped
2 garlic cloves, crushed
2 teaspoons grated fresh root ginger
1 teaspoon ground coriander
450 g/14½ oz chicken thighs, skinned, boned and cut into bite-sized pieces
250 ml/8 fl oz chicken stock
1 teaspoon garam masala
sea salt and pepper

This dish comes from southern India and should be eaten with rice and yogurt.

one Heat the oil in a large nonstick frying pan and, when hot, add the onion, curry leaves and chilli. Fry, stirring constantly, until the onions are soft. Add the garlic and ginger and stir-fry for 1–2 minutes.

two Add the ground coriander and chicken and fry, stirring constantly, for 2–3 minutes. Pour in the stock and add the garam masala. Cover and cook gently for 10–12 minutes, or until the chicken is cooked through. Season with salt and pepper and serve hot.

cashew nut chicken

1 onion, roughly chopped
4 tablespoons tomato purée
50 g/2 oz cashew nuts
2 teaspoons garam masala
2 garlic cloves, crushed
1 tablespoon lemon juice
¼ teaspoon ground turmeric
2 teaspoons sea salt
1 tablespoon natural yogurt
2 tablespoons vegetable oil
3 tablespoons chopped fresh coriander leaves
50 g/2 oz ready-to-eat dried apricots, chopped
500 g/1 lb chicken thighs, skinned, boned and cut into bite-sized pieces
300 ml/½ pint chicken stock
toasted cashew nuts and chopped fresh coriander, to garnish

Cashew nuts form the basis of this lovely thick and nutty curry.

one Put the onion, tomato purée, cashews, garam masala, garlic, lemon juice, turmeric, salt and yogurt into a food processor or blender and process until fairly smooth. Set aside.

two Heat the oil in a large nonstick frying pan and, when hot, pour in the spice mixture. Fry, stirring, for 2 minutes over a medium heat. Add half the coriander leaves, the apricots and chicken to the pan and stir-fry for 1 minute.

three Pour in the stock, cover and simmer for 10–12 minutes, or until the chicken is cooked through and tender. Stir in the remaining coriander leaves and serve garnished with toasted cashew nuts and chopped coriander.

Preparation time 10 minutes Cooking time 15 minutes Total time 25 minutes Serves 4

bombay chicken masala

1 onion, roughly chopped
6 fresh green chillies, deseeded and chopped
6 garlic cloves, chopped
2 teaspoons grated fresh root ginger
1 tablespoon ground coriander
2 teaspoons ground cumin
a large bunch of fresh coriander leaves,
roughly chopped
150 ml/¼ pint water
2 tablespoons vegetable oil
400 g/13 oz boneless chicken breast, cut into
strips
250 ml/8 fl oz chicken stock
sea salt and pepper

This is an excellent dish for a family supper or a mid-week meal with friends.

one Put the onion, chillies, garlic, ginger, ground coriander, cumin, coriander leaves and water in a food processor or blender process to a fairly smooth green paste. Set aside.

two Heat the oil in a large nonstick frying pan and add the green paste. Fry, stirring constantly, for 1 minute and then add the chicken. Fry, stirring, for 2–3 minutes, then add the stock. Mix well, cover and cook gently for 10–12 minutes, or until the chicken is tender. Season with salt and pepper and serve hot.

Preparation time 10 minutes Cooking time 12-15 minutes Total time 22-25 minutes Serves 4

chicken achaari

2 tablespoons vegetable oil
½ teaspoon cumin seeds
½ teaspoon black mustard seeds
½ teaspoon onion seeds
½ teaspoon fennel seeds
½ teaspoon coriander seeds
1 teaspoon grated fresh root ginger
2 garlic cloves, finely chopped
1 onion, finely chopped
1 teaspoon chilli powder
200 ml/7 fl oz chicken stock
2 tablespoons tomato purée
250 g/8 oz chicken thighs, skinned, boned and cut into bite-sized pieces
sea salt and pepper
chopped fresh red chillies, to garnish

The spices used in this dish are usually associated with making pickles 'achaar' hence the name.

one Heat the oil in a wok or large frying pan. When hot, add the cumin, mustard seeds, onion seeds, fennel and coriander seeds and stir-fry for 1 minute.

two Add the ginger, garlic, onion, chilli powder, stock and tomato purée and stir for 1 minute.

three Add the chicken and bring to the boil. Lower the heat, cover the pan and simmer for 5–7 minutes, or until the chicken is tender and cooked through. Season with salt and pepper and garnish with the chopped chillies.

Preparation time 10 minutes Cooking time 20 minutes Total time 30 minutes Serves 4

coconut chicken

1 tablespoon ground almonds
1 tablespoon desiccated coconut
125 ml/4 fl oz coconut milk
150 ml/¼ pint fromage frais
2 teaspoons ground coriander
1 teaspoon chilli powder
2 garlic cloves, crushed
2 teaspoons grated fresh root ginger
2 teaspoons sea salt
1 tablespoon vegetable oil
400 g/13 oz chicken thighs, skinned, boned and cut into bite-sized pieces
4 cardamom pods
1 teaspoon crushed red chilli flakes
3 tablespoons chopped fresh coriander
plain boiled rice, to serve

Both coconut milk and flesh enrich the flavour of this delicately spiced dish.

one In a small frying pan, dry-fry the almonds and coconut, stirring constantly, until light brown. Transfer to a mixing bowl and add the coconut milk, fromage frais, ground coriander, chilli powder, garlic, ginger and salt. Stir to mix well.

two Heat the oil in a large nonstick frying pan and sauté the chicken and cardamom for 2–3 minutes.

three Stir in the coconut mixture and chilli flakes, cover and cook gently for 10–12 minutes, stirring occasionally. Add the chopped coriander, stir and serve hot, with plain boiled rice.

Preparation time 10 minutes Cooking time 15–20 minutes Total time 25–30 minutes Serves 4

kheema aloo

1 tablespoon vegetable oil
4 cardamom pods
1 cinnamon stick
3 cloves
2 onions, finely chopped
375 g/12 oz minced lamb
2 teaspoons garam masala
2 teaspoons chilli powder
2 garlic cloves, crushed
2 teaspoons grated fresh root ginger
2 teaspoons sea salt
200 g/7 oz potatoes, cut into
1 cm/½ inch cubes
200 g/7 oz can chopped tomatoes
100 ml/3½ fl oz hot water
4 tablespoons chopped fresh coriander leaves
boiled rice or bread, to serve

This spicy, minced lamb dish with potatoes is gently flavoured with cardamom, cinnamon and cloves. Minced lamb may be replaced with minced chicken or pork, if liked.

one Heat the oil in a nonstick frying pan and, when hot, add the cardamom pods, cinnamon and cloves. Fry for 1 minute and then add the onion and fry, stirring, for 3–4 minutes.

two Add the lamb to the pan with the garam masala, chilli powder, garlic, ginger and salt. Stir well to break up the mince and fry for 5–7 minutes.

three Add the potatoes, tomatoes and the measured hot water, cover and simmer gently for 5 minutes, or until the potatoes are tender. Stir in the coriander and serve hot with rice.

Preparation time 10 minutes, plus chilling (optional)

Cooking time 10 minutes Total time 20 minutes Makes 12

seekh kebabs

2 fresh green chillies, deseeded and finely chopped
1 teaspoon grated fresh root ginger
2 garlic cloves, crushed
3 tablespoons chopped fresh coriander leaves
2 tablespoons chopped mint leaves
1 teaspoon cumin seeds
1 tablespoon vegetable oil
½ teaspoon ground cloves
½ teaspoon ground cardamom seeds
450 g/14½ oz minced beef
sea salt

These kebabs are a popular street food in India. Barbecued over charcoal braziers, they are eaten with red onions, mint and hot bread.

one Put the chillies, ginger, garlic, coriander leaves, mint, cumin, oil, ground cloves and cardamom into a food processor or blender and process until fairly smooth. Transfer to a mixing bowl, add the beef and salt and mix well, using your hands. Divide the mixture into 12 portions, cover and chill for 30 minutes, if time allows.

two Lightly oil 12 flat metal skewers and shape the kebab mixture around each skewer, forming a sausage shape.

three Place the kebabs under a preheated hot grill and cook for 3–4 minutes on each side, or until cooked through and browned.

Preparation time 10 minutes, plus marinating (optional)

Cooking time 8–12 minutes Total time 18–22 minutes Serves 4

kashmiri lamb chops

150 ml/¼ pint natural yogurt
1 teaspoon chilli powder
2 teaspoons grated fresh root ginger
2 garlic cloves, crushed
1 tablespoon sunflower oil, plus extra for greasing
8 lamb loin chops
sea salt and pepper

one Mix together the yogurt, chilli powder, ginger, garlic and oil in a large bowl and season with salt and pepper.

two Add the chops to this mixture and coat them thoroughly. Cover and marinate for 3–10 hours in the refrigerator, if time allows.

three Place the chops on a lightly oiled grill pan. Cook under a preheated hot grill for 4–6 minutes on each side, or until tender.

Preparation time 10 minutes Cooking time 20 minutes Total time 30 minutes Makes 12

lamb kebabs

450 g/14½ oz minced lamb
1 small red onion, finely chopped
3 tablespoons chopped fresh coriander leaves
2 tablespoons chopped mint leaves
2 fresh green chillies, chopped
2 garlic cloves, crushed
2 teaspoons grated fresh root ginger
1 egg, lightly beaten
sea salt and pepper

These kebabs are a spicy alternative to the hamburger. They work wonderfully stuffed in pitta bread with salad and could be cooked on a barbecue.

one Line a baking sheet with baking paper and set aside.

two Place the lamb, onion, coriander, mint, chillies, garlic, ginger and egg in a large bowl, season with salt and pepper and, using your hands, mix until thoroughly blended. Divide the mixture into 12 portions and form each one into a round shape.

three Place the kebabs on the baking sheet and bake in a preheated oven, 200°C (400°F), Gas Mark 6, for 20 minutes, or until golden brown. Serve hot.

beef chilli fry

3 tablespoons vegetable oil
6 large fresh green chillies, slit in half
1 teaspoon cumin seeds
4 curry leaves
2 teaspoons grated fresh root ginger
1 teaspoon chilli powder
1 teaspoon ground coriander
2 garlic cloves, crushed
2 teaspoons sea salt
2 onions, finely chopped
450 g/14½ oz beef sirloin steak, cut into thin strips
4 tablespoons lemon juice
2 tablespoons chopped mint
1 tablespoon chopped fresh coriander

one Heat the oil in a large nonstick frying pan and, when hot, add the chillies. Fry for 1 minute and then remove with a slotted spoon and set aside.

two Add the cumin, curry leaves, ginger, chilli powder, ground coriander, garlic, salt and onions to the pan and stir-fry for 1–2 minutes, stirring continuously.

three Add the beef strips and stir-fry for 8–10 minutes, until cooked through.

four Add the lemon juice, mint and chopped coriander, return the green chillies to the pan and fry, stirring, for 1–2 minutes. Serve immediately.

Preparation time 10 minutes, plus chilling **Cooking time** 6–8 minutes

Total time 16-18 minutes **Makes** 12

spicy pork patties

450 g/14½ oz minced pork
3 teaspoons hot curry paste
3 tablespoons fresh breadcrumbs
1 small onion, finely chopped
2 tablespoons lime juice
2 tablespoons chopped fresh coriander
1 fresh red chilli, finely chopped
2 teaspoons soft brown sugar
sunflower oil
sea salt and pepper
To serve:
natural yogurt
kachumber (see page 37)

one Put the pork, curry paste, breadcrumbs, onion, lime juice, coriander, chilli and sugar into a large bowl and, using your hands, mix until thoroughly blended. Season with salt and pepper, cover and chill for 30 minutes, or until ready to cook.

two Divide the mixture into 12 portions and shape each one into a flat round patty.

three Heat the oil in a large nonstick frying pan and cook the patties over a moderate heat for 3–4 minutes on each side, or until cooked through. Remove with a slotted spoon and drain on kitchen paper. Serve hot, with yogurt and kachumber.

fish & shellfish

Healthy, delicious and really quick to cook, these seafood recipes are influenced by the various different coastal regions of India.

Preparation time 10 minutes   Cooking time 15 minutes   Total time 25 minutes   Serves 4

salmon in banana leaves

a large bunch of fresh coriander, roughly chopped
3 tablespoons chopped mint leaves
2 garlic cloves, crushed
1 teaspoon grated fresh ginger root
4 fresh red chillies, chopped
2 teaspoons ground cumin
1 teaspoon ground coriander
2 teaspoons soft brown sugar
2 tablespoons lime juice
150 ml/¼ pint coconut milk
4 thick salmon fillets, skinned
4 squares of banana leaf (each approximately 30 x 30 cm/12 x 12 inches)
sea salt and pepper

All the aromas of the herbs and spices are unleashed when you open up the banana leaf packages.

one Place the chopped coriander, mint, garlic, ginger, chillies, cumin, ground coriander, sugar, lime juice and coconut milk in a food processor and blend until fairly smooth. Season with salt and pepper and set aside.

two Place each salmon fillet on a square of banana leaf and spoon some of the herb and spice mixture over it. Carefully cover the fish with the leaf to make a neat parcel and secure with wooden skewers.

three Place the parcels on a large baking sheet and bake in a preheated oven, 200°C (400°F), Gas Mark 6, for 15 minutes.

four Remove the parcels from the oven, place on a serving plate and open the packages at the table.

Tip: To make the banana leaves supple, hold them over an open flame until they go a bright green. They will be supple and easier to handle. If you cannot get hold of banana leaves, use baking paper instead.

Preparation time 10 minutes Cooking time 15–20 minutes Total time 25–30 minutes Serves 4

spicy pan-fried cod

2 tablespoons gram flour (besan)
1 tablespoon plain flour
1 tablespoon amchur (dried mango powder)
2 teaspoons chilli powder
1 tablespoon cumin seeds
1 teaspoon grated fresh root ginger
1 garlic clove, crushed
2 teaspoons sea salt
4 thick cod fillets, skinned
sunflower oil

In India, this dish would be prepared with a tropical fish, such as pomfret, but it is also a tasty way to cook cod.

one In a bowl, mix together the gram flour, plain flour, amchur, chilli powder, cumin seeds, ginger, garlic and salt.

two Place the fish on a chopping board and dust with the spiced flour on both sides, to coat evenly.

three Heat the oil in a large nonstick frying pan and, when hot, fry the fish in 2 batches, for 3–4 minutes on each side, or until cooked through. Drain on kitchen paper and serve hot.

Preparation time 10 minutes Cooking time 15 minutes Total time 25 minutes Serves 4

fish mollee

875 g/1¾ lb thick, skinless cod or halibut fillets, cut into 4 cm/1½ inch pieces
4 tablespoons lemon juice
1 tablespoon vegetable oil
1 onion, finely chopped
3 garlic cloves, crushed
1 teaspoon ground turmeric
4 fresh green chillies, deseeded and finely chopped
300 ml/½ pint coconut milk
1 tablespoon white wine vinegar
sea salt and pepper

This mild Anglo-Indian curry is wonderful served with boiled rice, Lime Pickle (see page 35) and poppadoms.

one Place the fish in a large, shallow non-metallic dish and sprinkle with salt and the lemon juice. Cover and set aside.

two Heat the oil in a large nonstick frying pan and add the onion and garlic. Fry, stirring constantly, for 2–3 minutes and then add the turmeric, chillies and coconut milk. Cook briskly for 2–3 minutes.

three Add the fish. Stir carefully and add the vinegar. Cover the pan and cook for 7–10 minutes, or until the fish is cooked through. Season with salt and pepper and serve hot.

Variation: Substitute raw tiger prawns for the fish. Cook until the prawns have just turned pink.

crab malabar-hill

2 tablespoons vegetable oil
3 garlic cloves, finely chopped
2 teaspoons finely chopped
fresh root ginger
6 spring onions, very thinly sliced
3 fresh red chillies, deseeded and finely sliced
625 g/1¼ lb fresh white crab meat
grated rind and juice of 1 lime
4 tablespoons chopped fresh coriander leaves
2 tablespoons chopped mint leaves
sea salt and pepper
lettuce leaves, to serve

This dish featured regularly on the menu at my home in Malabar-hill, Bombay.

one Heat the oil in a large wok or nonstick frying pan and, when hot, add the garlic, ginger, spring onions and chillies. Fry, stirring constantly, for 2–3 minutes.

two Add the crab meat, lime rind and juice, coriander and mint. Stir-fry for 2–3 minutes, season with salt and pepper and serve hot on crisp lettuce leaves.

Preparation time 10 minutes Cooking time 15 minutes Total time 25 minutes Serves 4

baked coconut trout

4 small trout, gutted and cleaned
4 tablespoons lemon juice
2 garlic cloves, crushed
1 teaspoon grated fresh root ginger
1 tablespoon ground almonds
3 tablespoons tomato purée
2 fresh green chillies, finely chopped
1 teaspoon garam masala
200 ml/7 fl oz coconut milk
1 tablespoon chopped fresh coriander leaves
1 tablespoon vegetable oil
sea salt and pepper
boiled rice and salad, to serve

one Place the fish in a large, non-metallic ovenproof dish, season with salt and squeeze over the lemon juice.

two Mix together the garlic, ginger, almonds, tomato purée, chillies, garam masala, coconut milk, coriander and oil. Season with salt and pepper and pour over the fish to coat well.

three Bake the fish in a preheated oven, 200°C (400°F), Gas Mark 6, for 15 minutes, until it is cooked through. Serve hot with rice and a salad.

Preparation time 10 minutes, plus marinating (optional)

Cooking time 12 minutes **Total time** 22 minutes **Serves** 4

kerala-style fried fish

1 small onion, finely grated to a paste
2 garlic cloves, finely grated
2 teaspoons ground coriander
1 teaspoon hot chilli powder
1 teaspoon pepper
1 tablespoon lemon juice
2 teaspoons sea salt
1 tablespoon sunflower oil, plus extra for frying
4 skinless plaice fillets
150 g/5 oz plain flour
sunflower oil, for frying

My idea of heaven would be sitting under the palms, by the sea, and making a meal of this fried fish, with dhal, rice and a salad.

one Place the onion, garlic, coriander, chilli powder, pepper, lemon juice, salt and the 1 tablespoon of oil in a bowl and mix thoroughly to form a paste. Place the fish in a large, non-metallic shallow dish and smear with the paste to coat evenly. Cover and marinate for 1 hour in the refrigerator, if time allows.

two Place the flour on a large plate and, when ready to cook, dredge the fish fillets in it. Shake off any excess flour.

three Heat the oil in a large nonstick frying pan and shallow-fry the fish, in batches, for about 2–3 minutes on each side. Drain on kitchen paper and serve hot.

Preparation time 10 minutes **Cooking time** 10–12 minutes **Total time** 20–22 minutes **Serves** 4

spiced mussel curry

1 kg/2 lb live mussels
1 tablespoon vegetable oil
1 onion, finely chopped
4 garlic cloves, crushed
3 fresh green chillies, finely chopped
1 teaspoon ground turmeric
100 ml/3½ fl oz white wine vinegar
400 ml/14 fl oz can coconut milk
2 teaspoons sugar
4 tablespoons chopped fresh coriander leaves
sea salt
freshly grated coconut, to garnish
crusty white bread, to serve

This is best made with live mussels, available from supermarkets and fishmongers.

one Rinse the mussels under cold, running water and scrape off any beards. Discard any that are open or that do not close when sharply tapped. Drain and set aside.

two Heat the oil in a large saucepan and add the onion, garlic, chillies and turmeric and fry for 2–3 minutes. Add the mussels, vinegar, coconut milk, sugar and chopped coriander. Stir well, bring to the boil, cover and cook gently for 5–6 minutes, or until all the mussels have opened. Discard any that remain shut.

three Transfer the mussels into a serving bowl with a slotted spoon, season to taste and pour over the mussels. Garnish with grated coconut and eat with crusty white bread to mop up the juices.

Preparation time 10 minutes Cooking time 12–15 minutes Total time 22–25 minutes Serves 4

prawns with curry leaves and fenugreek

1 tablespoon sunflower oil
2 onions, halved and thinly sliced
8–10 curry leaves
1 teaspoon nigella
1 fresh red chilli, finely sliced
625 g/1¼ lb raw tiger prawns, peeled and deveined
2 teaspoons grated fresh root ginger
2 teaspoons sea salt
1 tablespoon fenugreek leaves
1 tablespoon lemon juice
hot white bread, to serve

The marriage of the aromatic curry leaves and pungent fresh fenugreek leaves gives this prawn curry a distinctive flavour.

one Heat the oil in a large nonstick frying pan and add the onions, curry leaves and nigella and stir-fry for 3 minutes.

two Add the chilli and prawns and fry, stirring constantly, for 5–7 minutes. Add the ginger and salt and fry, stirring, for another minute, or until the prawns turn pink and are just cooked through.

three Finally, add the fenugreek leaves and lemon juice and cook for 1–2 minutes. Remove from the heat and serve hot with hot white bread.

Preparation time 10 minutes, plus marinating

Cooking time 8–10 minutes Total time 18–20 minutes Serves 4

monkfish kebabs

1 kg/2 lb monkfish fillet, cut into
4 cm/1½ inch cubes
200 ml/7 fl oz natural yogurt
4 tablespoons lemon juice
3 garlic cloves, crushed
2 teaspoons grated fresh root ginger
1 teaspoon hot chilli powder
1 teaspoon ground cumin
1 teaspoon ground coriander
2 fresh red chillies, finely sliced
sea salt and pepper
To garnish:
chopped fresh coriander
sliced red chillies
lime slices

Monkfish is quite meaty and holds its shape well when cooked, so it is perfect for kebabs.

one Place the monkfish cubes in a bowl and set aside.

two In a small bowl, mix together the yogurt, lemon juice, garlic, ginger, chilli powder, cumin, coriander and chillies and season with salt and pepper. Pour this over the fish, cover and marinate overnight.

three Lift the fish out of the marinade and thread on to 8 flat metal skewers. Place on a grill rack and cook under a preheated grill for 8–10 minutes, turning once, until the fish is cooked through. Serve hot and garnish with chopped coriander, lime slices and chilli slices.

Preparation time 10 minutes, plus marinating (optional)

Cooking time 20 minutes Total time 30 minutes Serves 4

baked spiced halibut

4 thick halibut steaks (about 200 g/7 oz each)
1 small onion, finely chopped
2 garlic cloves, crushed
1 teaspoon grated fresh root ginger
2 teaspoons ground cumin
1 teaspoon ground coriander
4 tablespoons lemon juice
1 teaspoon dried red chilli flakes
250 ml/8 fl oz natural yogurt
sea salt and pepper
To garnish
lemon wedges and coriander leaves

one Place the halibut steaks in a large, shallow ovenproof dish and set aside.

two Put the onion, garlic, ginger, cumin, coriander, lemon juice and chilli flakes in a food processor or blender with half the yogurt and process until smooth. Add the remaining yogurt and blend again. Season with salt and pepper.

three Pour the yogurt marinade over the fish, using your hands to coat the fish thoroughly on both sides. Cover and marinate in the refrigerator overnight, if time allows.

four Cover the dish with foil and bake in a preheated oven, 190°C (375°F), Gas Mark 5, for 10 minutes, then remove the foil and bake for another 7–10 minutes, or until the fish is cooked through. Serve hot, garnished with lemon wedges and coriander leaves.

Preparation time 10 minutes Cooking time 15 minutes Total time 25 minutes Serves 4

tomato fish curry

2 tablespoons vegetable oil
1 onion, finely chopped
4 garlic cloves, sliced
1 teaspoon grated fresh root ginger
½ teaspoon ground turmeric
1 teaspoon chilli powder
1 teaspoon ground cumin
2 teaspoons ground coriander
1 teaspoon garam masala
500 g/1 lb thick white fish fillets, cut into
2.5 cm/1 inch pieces
400 g/13 oz can chopped tomatoes
2 teaspoons sea salt
2 teaspoons sugar
boiled rice, to serve

Any firm white fish, such as cod or haddock, is suitable for this aromatic curry.

one Heat the oil in a large nonstick frying pan and fry the onion until soft and lightly browned. Add the garlic, ginger, turmeric, chilli powder, cumin, coriander and garam masala and fry for 30 seconds.

two Add the fish and stir gently for 1 minute.

three Add the tomatoes, salt and sugar, stir carefully, cover and simmer gently for 7–10 minutes, or until the fish is cooked through. Serve hot with rice.

Preparation time 10 minutes Cooking time 20 minutes Total time 30 minutes Serves 4

prawn dopiaza

2 tablespoons vegetable oil
3 onions, thinly sliced
1 teaspoon onion seeds
1 teaspoon grated garlic
1 teaspoon grated fresh root ginger
1 teaspoon chilli powder
½ teaspoon ground turmeric
625 g/1¼ lb raw tiger prawns, peeled and deveined
2 tablespoons fresh coriander leaves
1 tablespoon lemon juice
sea salt and pepper

Cooked with lots of onions – dopiaza – this dish has a rich and spicy flavour.

one Heat the oil in a large nonstick frying pan and add the onions. Cook over a medium heat, stirring occasionally, for about 7–10 minutes, until golden brown.

two Add the onion seeds, garlic, ginger, chilli powder and turmeric and stir-fry for 1–2 minutes.

three Add the prawns, coriander and lemon juice and season with salt and pepper. Cover the pan and cook gently for 5–7 minutes, or until the prawns are cooked through. Serve hot.

Preparation time 10 minutes   Cooking time 15 minutes   Total time 25 minutes   Serves 4

goan prawn curry

1 teaspoon chilli powder
1 tablespoon paprika
½ teaspoon ground turmeric
4 garlic cloves, crushed
2 teaspoons grated fresh root ginger
2 tablespoons ground coriander
1 teaspoon ground cumin
2 teaspoons jaggery or soft brown sugar
300 ml/½ pint water
400 ml/14 fl oz can coconut milk
2 teaspoons sea salt
1 tablespoon tamarind paste
625 g/1¼ lb raw tiger prawns
boiled white rice, to serve

I prepared a version of this extremely simple and wonderful recipe on a boat off the Goan coast, for one of Madhur Jaffrey's television series. I have cooked it regularly since then.

one Put the chilli powder, paprika, turmeric, garlic, ginger, ground coriander, cumin, the jaggery or brown sugar and the water in a bowl. Mix well and transfer to a large saucepan. Bring this mixture to the boil, cover and simmer gently for 7–8 minutes.

two Add the coconut milk, salt and tamarind paste and bring to a simmer.

three Stir in the prawns and cook briskly until they turn pink and are just cooked through. Serve hot, garnished with chopped coriander and accompanied by boiled white rice.

Tip: Peel and devein most of the prawns, leaving just the tail shell in place, but leave a few in their shells to improve the presentation of the dish.

vegetables & pulses

Fresh vegetables and pulses form the basis of day-to-day Indian cooking. A wide variety of common and slightly unusual vegetables are used in these recipes.

Preparation time 5 minutes, plus soaking

Cooking time 25 minutes Total time 30 minutes Serves 4

tarka dhal

250 g/8 oz red split lentils
1 litre/1¾ pints hot water
200 g/7 oz canned chopped tomatoes
2 fresh green chillies, deseeded and finely chopped (optional)
¼ teaspoon ground turmeric
2 teaspoons grated fresh root ginger
4 tablespoons chopped fresh coriander
sea salt and pepper
For the tarka:
1 tablespoon sunflower oil
2 teaspoons black mustard seeds
1 teaspoon cumin seeds
2 garlic cloves, thinly sliced
1 dried red chilli

This is the ultimate basic Indian comfort food. Tarka is the process by which food is given the final seasoning, in this case with spiced oil, to flavour the dish. I love to eat this dhal with basmati rice, natural yogurt and hot green mango pickle or Lime Pickle (see page 35).

one Soak the lentils in boiling water to cover for 10 minutes. Drain and put in a large saucepan with the hot water. Bring to the boil over a high heat, spooning off any scum that comes to the surface. Reduce the heat and cook for 20 minutes, or until soft and tender.

two Drain the lentils and process to a purée in a food processor or using a hand-held electric whisk. Return the purée to the rinsed pan with the tomatoes, chillies, turmeric, ginger and coriander. Season with salt and pepper, return to the heat and simmer gently.

three Meanwhile, make the tarka. Heat the oil in a small nonstick frying pan and, when hot, add all the ingredients and fry, stirring constantly, for 1–2 minutes.

four Remove the tarka from the heat and pour on to the cooked dhal. Stir and serve hot.

Preparation time 5 minutes Cooking time 20 minutes Total time 25 minutes Serves 4

spinach with besan

1 tablespoon vegetable oil
1 teaspoon mustard seeds
2 garlic cloves, finely chopped
250 g/8 oz baby spinach
1 teaspoon chilli powder
1 teaspoon ground cumin
2 teaspoons ground coriander
1 fresh green chilli, chopped
2 tablespoons gram flour (besan)
4 tablespoons water
dash of lemon juice
sea salt

one Heat the oil in a large frying pan and, when hot, add the mustard seeds, garlic and spinach. Sauté for 5 minutes and then add the chilli powder, cumin, coriander and chilli.

two Mix together the gram flour and water and pour into the spinach mixture. Stir and cook for 5 minutes, until the spinach and gram flour are well blended. Cover and cook gently for another 8–10 minutes.

three Season with salt and squeeze over some lemon juice. Serve hot.

Preparation time 10 minutes, plus resting

Cooking time 15–18 minutes Total time 25–28 minutes Serves 4

stuffed spiced okra

250 g/8 oz large fresh okra, trimmed
1 teaspoon grated fresh root ginger
1 teaspoon ground cumin
1 tablespoon amchur (dried mango powder)
½ teaspoon chilli powder
¼ teaspoon ground turmeric
2 teaspoons vegetable oil
3 tablespoons cornflour
sea salt and pepper
vegetable oil, for deep-frying

This unusual accompaniment would go down as well with Western grills as it does with other Indian dishes.

one With a sharp knife, make a lengthways slit in each okra, being careful not to cut right through.

two In a small bowl, mix together the ginger, cumin, amchur, chilli powder and turmeric. Add the oil, season with salt and pepper and stir to mix well. Set aside for 10–15 minutes to rest.

three Using your finger and a small teaspoon, carefully part the slits in the okra and fill each one with some of the spiced filling.

four Put the okra into a polythene bag with the cornflour and shake gently to coat them evenly.

five Pour at least 4 cm/1½ inches of oil into a wok or deep frying pan and heat. When hot, deep-fry the okra in 3 batches, for about 5–6 minutes, or until they are lightly browned and crisp. Drain on kitchen paper and serve hot.

mutter paneer

2 tablespoons vegetable oil
1 teaspoon mustard seeds
1 teaspoon cumin seeds
1 cinnamon stick or piece of cassia bark
1 dried red Kashmiri chilli
4 cloves
4 cardamom pods
1 onion, finely chopped
2 teaspoons freshly grated root ginger
1 fresh green chilli, chopped
4 garlic cloves, crushed
1 teaspoon hot chilli powder
1 teaspoon garam masala
1 teaspoon ground turmeric
2 tablespoons dhana-jeera
(see page 9)
2 teaspoons brown sugar or jaggery
200 g/7 oz can chopped tomatoes
200 g/7 oz paneer, cubed or crumbled
450 g/14½ oz frozen peas
175 ml/6 fl oz water
4 tablespoons crème fraîche
sea salt
fresh coriander leaves, to garnish

This famous, rich Moghul dish is wonderful when made with freshly made Paneer (see page 34). If pressed for time, you can use the shop-bought variety. Do not be intimidated by the long list of spices; if you have everything measured and laid out, it's simple.

one Heat the oil in a large saucepan and when hot, add the mustard and cumin seeds, cinnam on or cassia bark, dried red chilli, cloves and cardamom. Stir-fry until the seeds start to pop and then add the onion and stir-fry for 4–5 minutes. Add the ginger, chilli, garlic, chilli powder, garam masala, turmeric, dhanajeera and brown sugar and stir well.

two Add the tomatoes, paneer, peas and water. Simmer gently for 10 minutes, stirring occasionally.

three Stir in the crème fraîche and season with salt and pepper. Serve hot, garnished with coriander leaves.

coconut and potato curry

2 tablespoons vegetable oil
2 teaspoons black mustard seeds
¼ teaspoon asafoetida
8–10 curry leaves
1 teaspoon grated fresh root ginger
1 fresh green chilli, chopped
500 g/1 lb potatoes, cut into 2.5 cm/1 inch cubes and boiled
1 teaspoon hot chilli powder
1 tablespoon jaggery
200 ml/7 fl oz coconut milk
250 ml/8 fl oz water
1 tablespoon tamarind paste
2 tablespoons roasted cashew nuts, roughly chopped
3 tablespoons chopped fresh coriander
sea salt and pepper

This fragrant, sweet, sour and spicy curry is flavoured with tamarind paste, jaggery, asafoetida and curry leaves. If thinned down with some water, it also makes a great soup.

one Heat the oil in a large frying pan and, when hot, add the mustard seeds, asafoetida, curry leaves, ginger and chilli. Stir-fry for 1 minute and add the potatoes. Sauté for 1 minute.

two Sprinkle in the chilli powder and add the jaggery, coconut milk and measured water. Bring to the boil and add the tamarind paste and cashews. Lower the heat and simmer for 10–12 minutes. Stir in the coriander leaves, season with salt and pepper and serve hot.

Tip: If you cannot find jaggery – raw sugar produced by boiling down cane sugar juice – use brown sugar.

Preparation time 10 minutes Cooking time 20 minutes Total time 30 minutes Serves 4

oopma

175 g/6 oz coarse semolina
3 tablespoons vegetable oil
1 teaspoon black mustard seeds
1 teaspoon cumin seeds
1 dried red chilli, chopped
10-12 curry leaves
1 red onion, finely chopped
1 fresh green chilli, deseeded and chopped
50 g/2 oz raisins
2 tablespoons roasted cashew nuts
50 g/2 oz frozen peas
600 ml/1 pint hot water
1 tablespoon lemon juice
2 tablespoons freshly grated coconut
2 tablespoons chopped fresh coriander leaves
sea salt and pepper
To serve:
yogurt and cucumber
freshly grated coconut

Coarse semolina is used in this typical south Indian savoury breakfast treat. Do not buy the fine semolina used for puddings and sweets, or you will end up with a sticky mess. Coarse semolina is widely available from Indian or Asian stores. This would make a wonderful, spicy Sunday brunch.

one Heat a large heavy-based frying pan over a medium heat and dry-fry the semolina, stirring frequently, for 10 minutes, or until it turns golden brown. Set aside.

two Heat the oil in a large nonstick frying pan and, when hot, add the mustard seeds, cumin seeds, dried chilli and curry leaves. Stir-fry for 30 seconds, add the onion and green chilli and stir-fry until the onion has softened.

three Add the raisins, cashews, peas, semolina and water. Season with salt and pepper and cook over a low heat, stirring constantly, until the semolina has absorbed all the water. Stir in the lemon juice, coconut and coriander. Serve hot, with yogurt and cucumber, and freshly grated coconut.

Preparation time 10 minutes Cooking time 18-20 minutes Total time 28-30 minutes Serves 4

mushroom korma

2 tablespoons vegetable oil
1 onion, finely chopped
1 teaspoon grated fresh root ginger
1 fresh green chilli, chopped
500 g/1 lb large button or chestnut mushrooms, halved
1 teaspoon chilli powder
½ teaspoon ground turmeric
2 teaspoons ground cumin
1 tablespoon ground coriander
200 g/7 oz canned chopped tomatoes
1 teaspoon sugar
3 tablespoons single cream
2 tablespoons chopped fresh coriander leaves
sea salt and pepper

This is the perfect choice for those who love aromatic rather than fiery dishes.

one Heat the oil in a large saucepan and fry the onions until soft and lightly browned.

two Add the ginger, chilli and mushrooms and sauté for 5 minutes. Add the chilli powder, turmeric, cumin, coriander, tomatoes and sugar. Cover the saucepan and cook gently for about 8–10 minutes.

three Stir in the cream and chopped coriander, season with salt and pepper and serve hot.

Preparation time 10 minutes Cooking time 10 minutes Total time 20 minutes Serves 4

cabbage bhaji

500 g/1 lb white cabbage, roughly chopped
150 ml/¼ pint water
1 tablespoon vegetable oil
2 teaspoons urad dhal
1 teaspoon black mustard seeds
1 dried red chilli, finely chopped
6–8 curry leaves
2 tablespoons grated fresh coconut
sea salt

This cabbage dish uses urad dhal (a lentil), which has a nutty flavour when it is fried or roasted. It is used widely in many south Indian dishes.

one Place the cabbage in a large saucepan with the water, cover and cook over a medium heat for 10 minutes, stirring occasionally. Drain, return to the pan, set aside and keep warm.

two Meanwhile, heat the oil in a small nonstick frying pan and when hot, add the urad dhal, mustard seeds and dried chilli. Stir-fry for 1–2 minutes and, when the dhal turns light brown, add the curry leaves and fry, stirring constantly, for 2 minutes.

three Pour this spiced oil over the cabbage, stir in the coconut, season with salt and pepper and serve hot.

Preparation time 10 minutes Cooking time 10 minutes Total time 20 minutes Serves 4

jeera potatoes

2 tablespoons vegetable oil
1 tablespoon fresh root ginger, cut into fine slivers
1 tablespoon cumin seeds
500 g/1 lb potatoes, peeled, cut into 2.5 cm/1 inch cubes and boiled
1 fresh green chilli, finely sliced
2 teaspoons lime juice
sea salt and pepper
fresh coriander leaves, to garnish

Spiced with cumin, these potatoes go well with chicken and fish dishes.

one Heat the oil in a large frying pan and when hot, add the ginger and cumin. Stir-fry for 2 minutes, add the potatoes and chilli, season with salt and pepper and sauté for 6–8 minutes, or until the potatoes are lightly browned.

two Stir in the lime juice and sprinkle over the coriander leaves. Serve hot.

Preparation time 5 minutes Cooking time 20 minutes Total time 25 minutes Serves 4

spinach and chickpea sabzi

1 tablespoon vegetable oil
1 teaspoon cumin seeds
½ teaspoon coarsely ground coriander seeds
1 small onion, finely chopped
250 g/8 oz baby spinach
200 g/7 oz canned chopped tomatoes
1 teaspoon chilli powder
1 tablespoon dhana-jeera (see page 9)
1 teaspoon amchur (dried mango powder)
1 teaspoon jaggery or soft brown sugar
1 tablespoon lime juice
400 g/13 oz can chickpeas, rinsed and drained
175 ml/6 fl oz water
sea salt and pepper

This quick, tasty dish uses spinach and canned chickpeas, flavoured with dried mango powder (amchur).

one Heat the oil in a large frying pan and when hot add the cumin and coriander seeds and onion. Stir-fry until the onion is soft and light brown, then add the spinach and tomatoes and stir well.

two Add the chilli powder, dhanajeera, amchur, jaggery or sugar and lime juice and stir and cook for 1–2 minutes, then add the chickpeas and water. Season with salt and pepper, cover and simmer gently for 10 minutes, stirring occasionally. Serve hot.

Preparation time 10 minutes   Cooking time 10–12 minutes   Total time 20–22 minutes   Serves 4

brinjal and potato curry

1 small onion, chopped
2 teaspoons grated fresh root ginger
5 garlic cloves, roughly chopped
2 fresh green chillies, deseeded and chopped
100 ml/3½ fl oz water
4 tablespoons vegetable oil
1 large aubergine, cut into 1 cm/½ inch dice
500 g/1 lb potatoes, cut into 1 cm/½ inch cubes, boiled and drained
2 teaspoons cumin seeds
1 teaspoon nigella
1 teaspoon ground turmeric
1 teaspoon ground coriander
1 teaspoon ground cumin
1 tablespoon lemon juice
sea salt and pepper
chopped fresh coriander, to garnish

Aubergines (brinjal) cooked with potatoes and spices are wonderful stuffed into a sandwich or served with rice and Tarka Dhal (see page 79).

one Place the onion, ginger, garlic, chillies and water in a food processor or blender and process until smooth. Set aside.

two Heat 2 tablespoons of the oil in a large frying pan and, when hot, stir-fry the aubergine until lightly browned. Remove with a slotted spoon and set aside.

three Heat the remaining oil and, when hot, add the potatoes and cook until lightly browned. Remove with a slotted spoon and set aside.

four Add the cumin and nigella to the pan, stir for 30 seconds then add the turmeric, ground coriander, ground cumin and the onion paste. Fry for 2–3 minutes and then return the potatoes and aubergines to the pan. Season with salt and pepper and stir-fry for 3–4 minutes. Remove from the heat, stir in the lemon juice and serve hot, garnished with chopped coriander.

Preparation time 10 minutes   Cooking time 5–6 minutes   Total time 15–16 minutes   Serves 4

spiced beetroot

1 tablespoon vegetable oil
2 garlic cloves, finely chopped
1 teaspoon freshly grated ginger
1 teaspoon cumin seeds
1 teaspoon coriander seeds, roughly crushed
½ teaspoon dried red chilli flakes
625 g/1¼ lb freshly cooked and peeled beetroot, cut into wedges
150 ml/¼ pint coconut milk
¼ teaspoon ground cardamom seeds
grated rind and juice of 1 lime
handful of fresh chopped coriander
sea salt and pepper

Gently spiced with cardamom, coriander, cumin and lime, this dish will change the way you feel about this colourful, but humble root. Freshly cooked beetroot is now available everywhere; do not use those that have been preserved or cooked with vinegar.

one Heat the oil in a large frying pan and when hot, add the garlic, ginger, cumin, coriander seeds and chilli flakes. Stir-fry for 1–2 minutes then add the beetroot. Fry, stirring gently, for 1 minute and then add the coconut milk, ground cardamom, lime rind and juice and cook over a medium heat for 2–3 minutes.

two Stir in the chopped coriander, season with salt and pepper and serve hot, warm or at room temperature.

Preparation time 10 minutes   Cooking time 15 minutes   Total time 25 minutes   Serves 4

bhindi bhaji

3 tablespoons vegetable oil
1 teaspoon mustard seeds
1 teaspoon cumin seeds
500 g/1 lb okra, trimmed and cut into
1 cm/½ inch slices
1 teaspoon chilli powder
1 tablespoon dhana-jeera (see page 9)
2 teaspoons jaggery or soft brown sugar
1 tomato, finely chopped
2 tablespoons chopped fresh coriander leaves
sea salt and pepper
lime wedges, to serve

Okra is cooked in various different ways in India. It can be stuffed with a masala and fried, used in curries or finely sliced and deep-fried for a crunchy snack. Here it is quickly stir-fried.

one Heat the oil in a large frying pan and, when hot, add the mustard and cumin seeds. As soon as the mustard seeds begin to pop, add the okra and stir-fry for 8–10 minutes.

two Add the chilli powder, dhanajeera, jaggery and tomato and cook for another 3–5 minutes. Remove from the heat, season with salt and pepper and stir in the coriander leaves. Serve hot with lime wedges, to squeeze over.

Preparation time 10 minutes Cooking time 15–20 minutes Total time 25–30 minutes Serves 4

pumpkin curry

1 tablespoon vegetable oil
1 onion, halved and thinly sliced
4 garlic cloves, crushed
1 teaspoon ground cumin
2 teaspoons ground coriander
1 fresh green chilli, finely chopped
6 curry leaves
400 ml/14 fl oz can coconut milk
200 ml/7 fl oz hot water
750 g/1½ lb pumpkin, cut into 5 cm/2 inch cubes
sea salt and pepper
2 tablespoons chopped fresh coriander leaves

Coconut milk perfectly complements the spiced pumpkin.

one Heat the oil in a large saucepan and, when hot, add the onion and stir-fry until soft and lightly browned. Add the garlic, cumin, ground coriander, chilli and curry leaves and stir-fry for another minute.

two Pour in the coconut milk, hot water and pumpkin, bring to the boil, cover and simmer gently for 10–15 minutes, or until the pumpkin is tender.

three Season with salt and pepper and stir in the coriander leaves. Serve hot.

Preparation time 10 minutes Cooking time 8–10 minutes Total time 18–20 minutes Serves 4

mango curry

1 tablespoon vegetable oil
1 teaspoon mustard seeds
1 onion, halved and thinly sliced
15–20 curry leaves
½ teaspoon dried red chilli flakes
1 teaspoon grated fresh root ginger
1 fresh green chilli, deseeded and sliced
1 teaspoon ground turmeric
3 ripe mangoes, peeled, stoned and thinly sliced
400 ml/14 fl oz natural yogurt, lightly beaten
sea salt

Use really ripe mangoes to ensure a really fruity flavour.

one Heat the oil in a large saucepan and, when hot, add the mustard seeds, onion, curry leaves and dried chilli flakes. Fry, stirring, for 4–5 minutes, or until the onion is lightly browned.

two Add the ginger and green chilli to the onion mixture, stir-fry for 1 minute and add the turmeric. Stir to mix well then remove the saucepan from the heat.

three Add the mangoes and yogurt, stirring constantly, until well mixed. Season with salt, to taste. Return the saucepan to a low heat and cook for 1 minute, stirring constantly. (Do not let it boil or the curry will curdle.) Serve warm.

broccoli sabzi

2 tablespoons vegetable oil
1 teaspoon cumin seeds
1 onion, halved and finely sliced
1 fresh red chilli, finely sliced
3 garlic cloves, finely chopped
300 g/10 oz broccoli, cut into
bite-sized florets
sea salt and pepper

This delicately spiced dish makes a good accompaniment to a heavily spiced curry.

one Heat the oil in a large nonstick frying pan and, when hot, add the cumin. Stir-fry for 1 minute and then add the onion. Cook over a moderate heat until lightly browned.

two Stir in the chilli, garlic and broccoli. Cover the pan and reduce the heat to low. Cook for 6–8 minutes, until the broccoli is just tender. Season with salt and pepper and serve hot.

Preparation time 10 minutes Cooking time 18–20 minutes Total time 28–30 minutes Serves 4

shallot curry

2 tablespoons vegetable oil
1 teaspoon coarsely ground coriander seeds
1 teaspoon cumin seeds
3 plum tomatoes, roughly chopped
10 shallots, peeled
1 teaspoon chilli powder
½ teaspoon ground turmeric
1 tablespoon dhana-jeera powder (see page 9)
1 teaspoon sugar
4-6 tablespoons lemon juice
3 large potatoes, cut into matchsticks
150 ml/¼ pint water
2 tablespoons chopped fresh coriander leaves
sea salt and pepper

The delicate, sweet flavour of shallots is complemented by the aromatic spices in this flavoursome curry.

one Heat the oil in a large frying pan and, when hot, add the coriander and cumin seeds, tomatoes and shallots. Stir-fry for 2 minutes, then add the chilli powder, turmeric, dhanajeera powder, sugar and lemon juice to taste. Stir to mix well.

two Add the potatoes and water, cover and cook gently for 10–15 minutes, or until the potatoes are tender. Stir in the coriander leaves, season with salt and pepper and serve hot.

rice & breads

Delicious, aromatic and easy to make kitchere, coconut rice, naan bread and spiced puris.

Preparation time 5 minutes, plus soaking and standing

Cooking time 15 minutes Total time 20 minutes Serves 4

saffron and cardamom rice

15 g/½ oz unsalted butter
1 tablespoon vegetable oil
1 onion, finely chopped
2 dried red chillies
6 cardamom pods, lightly crushed
1 cinnamon stick
1 teaspoon cumin seeds
2 bay leaves
225 g/7½ oz basmati rice, washed and soaked
in cold water for 15 minutes
1 teaspoon saffron strands, soaked
in 1 tablespoon hot milk
475 ml/16 fl oz boiling water
sea salt and pepper
crispy fried onions, to garnish

Flavoured with the aromatic spices cardamom and saffron, this fragrant rice dish makes a delicious centrepiece for any Indian meal.

one Heat the butter and oil in a large heavy-based saucepan and add the onion. Stir and cook over a moderate heat for 2–3 minutes. Add the dried red chillies, cardamom pods, cinnamon, cumin seeds and bay leaves.

two Drain the rice, add to the pan and stir-fry for 2–3 minutes. Add the saffron mixture and boiling water, season with salt and pepper and bring back to the boil. Cover tightly, reduce the heat to low and simmer gently for 10 minutes. Do not lift the lid, as the steam is required for the cooking process.

three Remove the pan from the heat and leave the rice to stand, covered and undisturbed, for 8–10 minutes. Fluff up the grains with a fork and serve garnished with crispy fried onions.

Tip: To make crispy fried onions, thinly slice an onion and shallow-fry until crisp and golden. Drain on kitchen paper and serve sprinkled over rice dishes.

Preparation time 5 minutes, plus soaking and standing

Cooking time 15 minutes **Total time** 20 minutes **Serves** 4

tomato rice

25 g/1 oz butter
1 small onion, halved and thinly sliced
1 garlic clove, crushed
1 teaspoon cumin seeds
4–6 black peppercorns
1 clove
1 cinnamon stick
50 g/2 oz frozen peas
200 g/7 oz canned chopped tomatoes
2 tablespoons tomato purée
225 g/7½ oz basmati rice, washed and soaked
in cold water for 15 minutes
475 ml/16 fl oz boiling water
2 tablespoons chopped fresh coriander leaves
sea salt and pepper

This aromatic and delicately flavoured and coloured rice would make a good dinner party dish.

one Heat the butter in a large heavy-based saucepan and, when melted, add the onion, garlic, cumin, peppercorns, clove and cinnamon. Stir-fry for 2–3 minutes. Drain the rice.

two Add the peas, tomatoes, tomato purée and rice and stir-fry for another 2–3 minutes.

three Add the boiling water and coriander leaves, season with salt and pepper and bring back to the boil. Cover tightly, reduce the heat to low and simmer gently for 10 minutes. Do not lift the lid, as the steam is required for the cooking process.

four Remove the pan from the heat and leave the rice to stand, covered and undisturbed, for 8–10 minutes. To serve, fluff up the grains of rice with a fork.

Preparation time 5 minutes, plus soaking and standing

Cooking time 15 minutes Total time 30 minutes Serves 4

jeera rice

25 g/1 oz unsalted butter
2 teaspoons cumin seeds
1 clove
2 cardamom pods, lightly crushed
225 g/7½ oz basmati rice, washed and soaked in cold water for 15 minutes
475 ml/16 fl oz boiling water
sea salt and pepper

This simple rice dish, flavoured with cumin, makes a great accompaniment to any Indian meal.

one Melt the butter in a large heavy-based saucepan over a medium heat. Add the cumin seeds, clove and cardamom pods and stir-fry for 30 seconds.

two Drain the rice, add to the pan and stir to coat in the spiced butter for 2–3 minutes. Pour in the boiling water and bring back to the boil. Season with salt and pepper, stir, cover tightly and simmer over a low heat for 10 minutes. Do not lift the lid, as the steam is required for the cooking process.

three Remove the pan from the heat and leave the rice to stand, covered and undisturbed, for 8–10 minutes. To serve, lightly fluff up the grains with a fork.

Preparation time 5 minutes, plus soaking and standing

Cooking time 18–20 minutes Total time 23–25 minutes Serves 4

kitcheree

15 g/½ oz unsalted butter
1 tablespoon vegetable oil
1 onion, halved and thinly sliced
1 cinnamon stick
4–5 cloves
6 black peppercorns
1 teaspoon grated fresh root ginger
2 fresh green chillies, deseeded and finely chopped
1 teaspoon cumin seeds
2 teaspoons ground coriander
100 g/3½ oz dried moong dhal (split yellow lentils), rinsed and drained
225 g/7½ oz basmati rice, rinsed and soaked in cold water for 15 minutes
600 ml/1 pint boiling water
sea salt and pepper
To garnish
crispy fried onions and hard-boiled eggs

This traditional dish of rice cooked with lentils inspired the breakfast dish of the Raj – kedgeree.

one Heat the butter and oil in a large heavy-based saucepan and add the onion. Cook until lightly browned and add the cinnamon, cloves, peppercorns, ginger, chillies, cumin seeds, ground coriander, moong dhal and rice. Season with salt and pepper and stir-fry for 3–4 minutes.

two Add the boiling water and bring back to the boil. Cover the pan tightly, reduce the heat to low and cook for 10 minutes. Do not lift the lid, as the steam is required for the cooking process. Remove the pan from the heat and leave to stand, covered and undisturbed, for 8–10 minutes.

three To serve, fluff up the grains of rice with a fork and garnish with crispy fried onions and hard-boiled eggs.

Preparation time 5 minutes, plus soaking and standing

Cooking time 15 minutes **Total time** 20 minutes **Serves** 4

coconut rice

2 tablespoons vegetable oil
2 teaspoons black mustard seeds
1 teaspoon cumin seeds
10 curry leaves
1 dried red chilli, finely chopped
225 g/7½ oz basmati rice, washed and soaked
in cold water for 15 minutes
100 ml/3½ fl oz coconut milk
375 ml/13 fl oz boiling water
sea salt and pepper
roasted cashew nuts, to garnish

Lightly spiced and fragrant with coconut milk, this rice dish is the perfect partner for fish or seafood.

one Heat the oil in a large heavy-based saucepan and, when hot, add the mustard seeds, cumin, curry leaves and dried chilli.

two Drain the rice, add to the pan and stir-fry for 1–2 minutes. Add the coconut milk and boiling water, season with salt and pepper and bring back to the boil. Cover tightly, reduce the heat to low and simmer gently for 10–12 minutes. Do not lift the lid, as the steam is required for the cooking process.

three Remove the pan from the heat and leave to stand, covered and undisturbed, for 8–10 minutes. To serve, fluff up the grains of rice with a fork and garnish with roasted cashew nuts.

Preparation time 10 minutes, plus standing

Cooking time 18–20 minutes Total time 28–30 minutes Serves 4

mushroom pulao

25 g/1 oz unsalted butter
3–4 garlic cloves, thinly sliced
1 teaspoon grated fresh root ginger
3 spring onions, thinly sliced
½ teaspoon ground turmeric
250 g/8 oz chestnut mushrooms, thinly sliced
225 g/7½ oz easy-cook basmati rice, rinsed and drained
2 tablespoons chopped fresh coriander leaves
600 ml/1 pint boiling vegetable stock or water
sea salt and pepper

This dish uses easy-cook basmati rice, combined with mushrooms, spring onions, herbs and spices. The rice needs no soaking.

one Heat the butter in a large heavy-based saucepan and, when melted, add the garlic, ginger, spring onions, turmeric, mushrooms and rice. Stir-fry for 2–3 minutes and then add the chopped coriander. Season with salt and pepper and pour in the boiling stock or water. Bring back to the boil, cover the pan tightly, reduce the heat to low and simmer for 15 minutes. Do not lift the lid, as the steam is required for the cooking process.

two Remove the pan from the heat and leave to stand, covered and undisturbed, for 8–10 minutes. To serve, fluff the grains of rice with a fork.

Preparation time 5 minutes, plus standing

Cooking time 15–18 minutes Total time 20–23 minutes Serves 4

spinach and chickpea pulao

15 g/½ oz unsalted butter
1 tablespoon vegetable oil
1 onion, finely chopped
1 teaspoon cumin seeds
2 teaspoons ground coriander
2 garlic cloves, crushed
1 teaspoon grated fresh root ginger
100 g/3½ oz spinach leaves, finely shredded
400 g/13 oz can chickpeas, rinsed and drained
225 g/7½ oz easy-cook basmati rice, rinsed and drained
2 tablespoons chopped dill
600 ml/1 pint boiling vegetable stock
sea salt and pepper

one Heat the butter and oil in a large heavy-based frying pan and, when hot, add the onion. Cook over a moderate heat until lightly browned, then add the cumin seeds, ground coriander, garlic, ginger, spinach, chickpeas, rice and dill. Stir and season with salt and pepper.

two Pour over the boiling stock and bring back to the boil. Cover the pan tightly, reduce the heat to low and cook gently for 10–12 minutes. Do not lift the lid, as the steam is required for the cooking process.

three Remove the pan from the heat and leave the rice to stand, covered and undisturbed, for 8–10 minutes. Fluff up the grains with a fork and serve hot.

naan

225 g/7½ oz self-raising flour
5 g/¼ oz sachet easy-blend dried yeast
1 teaspoon sea salt
1 teaspoon roasted cumin seeds
2 tablespoons natural yogurt, lightly beaten
1 tablespoon melted butter, plus extra for brushing
4 tablespoons lukewarm milk
fresh coriander leaves, to garnish

Though readily available in supermarkets and shops, there is nothing like freshly made naan bread. You can also vary the flavourings used when you make your own.

one In a large, warmed mixing bowl, mix together the flour, yeast, salt, cumin seeds, yogurt and butter. Add the milk and knead to make a soft dough. Cover with a lightly oiled sheet of polythene and leave to rest for 20–25 minutes in a warm (not hot) place.

two Turn the dough out on to a large board or surface, lightly dusted with flour, and knead for 3–4 minutes, or until smooth. Divide the dough into 8 portions and roll each one up into a ball.

three With a rolling pin, roll each ball out into an oval or triangular shape, the size of a pitta bread.

four Brush with melted butter and cook in batches, under a preheated hot grill, for 2–3 minutes on each side. Serve hot, garnished with coriander leaves.

Tip: Instead of the cumin seeds, you can use 1 teaspoon nigellas, poppy seeds, sesame seeds, or 2 finely chopped garlic cloves.

Preparation time 10 minutes, plus resting

Cooking time 10 minutes Total time 20 minutes Makes 10

bhaturas

175 g/6 oz self-raising flour
1 tablespoon oil
1 tablespoon natural yogurt
1 teaspoon sea salt
2–3 tablespoons water
oil, for deep-frying

Quick and easy to prepare, these deep-fried puris (puffed up bread) are excellent served with Jeera Potatoes (see page 85), Brinjal and Potato Curry (see page 87) or Prawns with Curry Leaves and Fenugreek (see page 69).

one In a large mixing bowl, combine the flour, oil, yogurt and salt. Mix well and add enough water to make a soft dough. Cover with a tea towel and allow to rest for 15 minutes.

two Turn the dough out on to a lightly floured board and knead well for 3–4 minutes, or until smooth. Divide the mixture into 10 portions and roll up each portion into a ball.

three Using a rolling pin, roll each ball into an 8 cm/3½ inch disc and set aside.

four Heat the oil for deep-frying in a large wok or deep frying pan to 180–190°C (350–375°F) or until a cube of bread browns in 30 seconds. Carefully slide 2–3 bhaturas into the wok. When the bhaturas puff up, turn them over and cook for 1 minute, or until lightly browned on both sides. Carefully remove with a slotted spoon and drain on kitchen paper. Repeat until all the bhaturas are fried and serve immediately

Preparation time 10 minutes Cooking time 20 minutes Total time 30 minutes Makes 16

spiced puris

225 g/7½ oz atta or chapatti flour
1 teaspoon hot chilli powder
1 teaspoon cumin seeds
½ teaspoon ground turmeric
1 teaspoon sea salt
1–2 tablespoons water
oil, for deep-frying

These puris make a quick and tasty snack. They are made with atta or chapatti flour, a medium-grade wheat flour that is sold in Indian and Asian shops.

one Put the flour, chilli powder, cumin, turmeric and salt in a large mixing bowl and add enough water to make a soft, but not sticky dough. Knead until the dough is smooth and elastic.

two Divide the dough into 16 portions and roll each one out to an 8 cm/3½ inch disc.

three Heat the oil in a large wok or deep frying pan to 180–190°C (350–375°F) or until a cube of bread browns in 30 seconds. Fry the puris in batches of 2 or 3. The puris will puff up and, when they do, turn them over until browned and crisp. Remove with a slotted spoon and drain on kitchen paper. Serve hot or at room temperature. They will keep for up to a week, if stored in an airtight container.

desserts

Indian desserts are usually
served on special religious
and festive occasions.
However, these gently
flavoured and lightly spiced
desserts are ideal for everyday
cooking and entertaining.

Preparation time 5 minutes, plus chilling (optional) Total time 5 minutes Serves 4

shrikandh

500 g/1 lb curd cheese
125 g/4 oz cream cheese
150 g/5 oz natural yogurt
3 tablespoons caster sugar
1 tablespoon rosewater
2 teaspoons crushed cardamom seeds
1 teaspoon saffron strands, soaked
in 1 tablespoon hot water
chopped pistachio nuts and rose petals, to
decorate

This dessert, made with curd cheese and flavoured with cardamom and saffron, was one of my childhood favourites. It is really scrumptious when eaten with freshly made puris.

one In a large mixing bowl, beat together the cheeses, yogurt, sugar, rosewater and cardamom, until smooth and glossy.

two Stir in the saffron mixture, mix well and chill for a couple of hours, if time allows.

three To serve, sprinkle over finely chopped pistachios and rose petals.

Preparation time 10 minutes Cooking time 10–15 minutes Total time 25-30 minutes Serves 4

banana and cardamom pancakes

4 ripe bananas, mashed
300 g/10 oz self-raising flour
2 tablespoons caster sugar
2 tablespoons melted butter
100 ml/3½ fl oz milk
1 egg, lightly beaten
2 teaspoons crushed cardamom seeds
sunflower oil
To serve
vanilla ice cream and honey

Banana and cardamom are an unbeatable combination, so these pancakes are sure to become a family favourite.

one Put the bananas, flour, sugar, butter, milk and egg in a large mixing bowl and whisk until smooth. Stir in the cardamom seeds.

two Heat a large nonstick frying pan and brush with the oil. Pour in 3–4 tablespoonfuls of batter and let cook for 2–3 minutes. Flip the pancakes over and cook for a futher 2 minutes, or until lightly browned and cooked through. Remove the pancakes with a slotted spoon and keep warm. Repeat with the remaining batter, until all the pancakes are cooked.

three Serve 2–3 pancakes per person, with vanilla ice cream and honey.

Preparation time 10 minutes, plus chilling Total time 10 minutes Serves 4

mango fool

3 ripe mangoes, stoned, pitted and chopped
juice and finely grated rind of 1 lime
2 teaspoons soft brown sugar
250 ml/8 fl oz double cream, lightly whipped
diced mango, to decorate

Always try to use the ripest mangoes available.

one Put the mangoes, lime juice and rind and sugar in a food processor or blender and process until smooth. Transfer to a large mixing bowl, fold in the whipped cream and mix well.

two Pour the fool into 4 dessert glasses, cover and chill for 3–4 hours, until ready to serve. Garnish with diced mango.

Preparation time 10 minutes, plus chilling (optional)

Cooking time 18–20 minutes **Total time** 28–30 minutes **Makes** 12–15 squares

coconut barfi

400 g/13 oz caster sugar
450 ml/¾ pint boiling water
4 tablespoons butter
250 g/8 oz grated fresh coconut
2 teaspoons crushed cardamom seeds
100 g/3½ oz pistachio nuts, roughly chopped,
plus extra to decorate

This delicious coconut fudge, is easy to make and will keep in an airtight container for up to one week, if it hasn't all been eaten by then.

one Place the sugar in a large heavy-based saucepan with the boiling water and bring back to the boil. Cook over a medium heat for 8–10 minutes, or until the syrup is reduced and thick.

two Stir in the butter, coconut and cardamom seeds and cook for another 10 minutes, stirring constantly. Remove from the heat and stir in the pistachios.

three Pour the mixture into a lightly greased Swiss roll tin (about 30 x 20 cm/12 x 8 inches), spread evenly and, when cool, chill for 6 hours, if time allows. To serve, cut the barfi into squares and garnish with extra chopped pistachios.

spiced caramelized pears with ginger cream

200 ml/7 fl oz double cream, lightly whipped
2 pieces stem ginger in syrup, finely chopped
1 tablespoon syrup from the jar of stem
ginger
For the pears:
2 tablespoons butter
4-5 firm dessert pears, peeled, cored and cut
into thick slices
75 g/3 oz caster sugar
¼ teaspoon ground cinnamon
a pinch of ground cloves
½ teaspoon crushed cardamom seeds
100 g/3½ oz chopped walnuts

A sophisticated, but easy dessert that is ideal for a dinner party.

one Make the ginger cream by mixing the cream, stem ginger and ginger syrup together in a bowl. Cover and chill until ready to serve.

two Melt the butter in a large nonstick frying pan and add the pears, sugar, cinnamom, cloves, cardamom seeds and walnuts and cook over a medium heat for 3-4 minutes, stirring occasionally.

three Increase the heat to high and cook for 6-8 minutes, stirring occasionally, until the pears are lightly caramelized. Serve hot, with tablespoonfuls of the ginger cream.

Preparation time 5 minutes Cooking time 25 minutes Total time 30 minutes Serves 4

gajjar halwa

750 ml/1¼ pints full fat milk
300 g/10 oz carrots, roughly grated
40 g/1½ oz butter
1 tablespoon golden syrup
125 g/4 oz caster sugar
50 g/2 oz sultanas or golden raisins
1 teaspoon crushed cardamom seeds
To serve:
finely flaked almonds
vanilla ice cream or whipped cream

This rich and luscious dessert, made with carrots, is almost fudge-like in texture. Served warm with ice cream, who could ask for anything more?

one Put the milk, carrots, butter, golden syrup, sugar, sultanas and cardamom in a large, heavy-based saucepan. Bring to the boil and cook over a moderate heat for 20 minutes, stirring often, until all the liquid has been absorbed and the mixture has thickened.

two Spread the halwa into a shallow dish and leave to stand until ready to serve.

three Sprinkle the flaked almonds over the halwa and serve with scoops of vanilla ice cream or whipped cream.

Preparation time 5 minutes Cooking time 15 minutes Total time 20 minutes Serves 4

seviyan

25 g/1 oz butter
100 g/3½ oz dried vermicelli
400 ml/14 fl oz milk
200 ml/7 fl oz water
pinch of saffron strands
150 g/5 oz caster sugar
50 g/2 oz flaked, toasted almonds
½ teaspoon crushed cardamom seeds

This traditional dessert is made with vermicelli. Use the vermicelli found in Asian greengrocers, as it is a finer variety.

one Heat the butter in a large saucepan and, when melted, add the vermicelli, breaking it into smaller pieces. Fry, stirring, until the vermicelli turns light brown.

two Pour the milk and water into the saucepan with the saffron. Mix well and bring to the boil. Continue to boil for 8–10 minutes and then add the sugar. Reduce the heat to medium, cover the pan, and cook until the vermicelli is cooked and most of the liquid has been absorbed.

three Stir in the almonds and cardamom and serve hot or chilled.

Preparation time 15 minutes Cooking time 15 minutes Total time 30 minutes Makes 12

chocolate and banana samosas

2 ripe bananas, roughly mashed
1 tablespoon dark chocolate chips
12 filo pastry sheets, each about 30 x 18 cm
(12 x 7 inches)
melted butter, for brushing
icing sugar, for dusting

These sweet samosas are delicious hot, straight from the oven. Serve with lightly whipped cream or ice cream.

one Mix the banana with the chocolate chips and set aside.

two Fold each sheet of filo pastry in half lengthways. Place a large spoonful of the banana mixture at one end of the filo strip and then fold the corner of the filo over the mixture, covering it in a triangular shape. Continue folding the pastry over and over along the length of the strip of pastry to make a neat triangular samosa. Moisten the edge with water to seal and place on a baking baking sheet lined with baking paper. Repeat with the remaining filling and pastry.

three Brush the samosas with melted butter and bake in a preheated oven, 180°C (350°F), Gas Mark 4, for 12–15 minutes, or until lightly golden and crisp. Remove from the oven, dust with icing sugar and serve hot.

Tip: When working with filo pastry, always keep the pastry covered with a damp tea towel to prevent it from drying out, until ready to use.

Preparation time 5 minutes, plus chilling (optional)

Cooking time 25 minutes **Total time** 30 minutes **Serves** 4

kheer

100 g/3½ oz Thai jasmine rice
750 ml/1¼ pints full-fat milk
3 tablespoons caster sugar
½ teaspoon grated nutmeg
1 teaspoon crushed cardamom seeds
50 g/2 oz pistachio nuts, chopped, plus extra
to garnish
varq (silver leaf), to garnish (optional)

This Indian version of rice pudding is delicately flavoured with nutmeg, cardamom and pistachio nuts. I use Thai jasmine rice which results in a creamier texture. Serve chilled.

one Put the rice, milk and sugar in a large heavy-based saucepan and bring to the boil. Lower the heat and simmer for 10 minutes. Add the nutmeg, cardamom and pistachios and continue to cook for a further 10 minutes, stirring often, until the mixture is thick and creamy.

two Pour into 4 serving bowls, cover and chill for at least 6 hours before serving, if time allows. Garnish with pistachios and varq, if liked.

drinks & coolers

Tropical and exotic fruits and spices such as mango, watermelon, lemongrass and cardamom flavour these delicious hot and cold beverages.

Preparation time 10 minutes Total time 10 minutes **Serves** 4

mango lassi

3 fresh ripe mangoes, peeled, stoned and
roughly chopped, or 300 ml/½ pint tinned
mango pulp
500 ml/17 fl oz yogurt
250 mls 8 fl oz water
1–2 tablespoons caster sugar

one Put the fresh mango in a blender or food processor and blend until smooth. Set
aside.

two Blend the yogurt, water and sugar in a food processor until smooth. Divide the
mango pulp between 4 tall glasses and pour over the yogurt mixture.
Serve chilled.

Preparation time 10 minutes Total time 10 minutes Serves 4

kesar cooler

1 tablespoon ground almonds
1 teaspoon saffron strands
1 tablespoon chopped pistachio nuts, plus
extra to decorate
½ teaspoon crushed cardamom pods
2 tablespoons caster sugar
1 litre/1¾ pints cold milk
2–3 scoops vanilla ice cream

A version of this chilled, saffron-flavoured milkshake is usually made on festive occassions.

one Put the almonds, saffron, pistachio nuts, cardamom and sugar in a mortar, add 3 tablespoons hot water and, using a pestle, grind well to make a paste.

two Transfer this paste to a food processor or blender and add the milk and ice cream. Blend well, until smooth.

three Pour into chilled glasses and serve decorated with some chopped pistachio nuts.

Preparation time 10 minutes Total time 10 minutes Serves 4

banana lassi

3 ripe bananas, roughly chopped
500 ml/17 fl oz natural yoghurt
250 ml/8 fl oz cold water
1–2 tablespoons caster sugar
¼ teaspoon ground cardamom seeds

This is an ideal breakfast drink.

one Put all the ingredients in a food processor or blender and blend until smooth. Pour into tall glasses and serve chilled.

Preparation time 10 minutes, plus chilling (optional) Total time 10 minutes Serves 4–6

watermelon cooler

1 large, ripe watermelon
pinch of salt
a few mint leaves to decorate

one Peel and deseed the watermelon and cut into cubes. Place in a food processor or blender (you might have to do this in 2 batches) and blend until fairly smooth. Transfer to a large jug and add a pinch of salt. Stir to mix well and chill, covered, for 3–4 hours before serving.

two Serve in tall glasses with mint leaves, to decorate.

Preparation time 5 minutes Total time 5 minutes Serves 4

mango and mint sherbet

3 ripe mangoes, peeled, stoned and
roughly chopped
4 tablespoons lemon juice
1 tablespoon caster sugar
12 mint leaves, finely chopped
900 ml/1½ pints ice cold water
ice cubes

one Put the mango, lemon juice, sugar and mint leaves in a food processor or blender with the water and blend until smooth. To serve, pour into ice-filled glasses.

Preparation time 10 minutes Cooking time 10 minutes Total time 20 minutes Serves 4

masala chai

6 teaspoons Darjeeling tea leaves
200 ml/7 fl oz milk
¼ teaspoon ground ginger
¼ teaspoon crushed cardamom seeds
⅛ teaspoon ground cloves
1 cinnamon stick
1 tablespoon caster sugar
900 ml/1½ water

This milky tea, lightly spiced with ginger, cardamom, cloves and cinnamon, is drunk all over India.

one Put all the ingredients into a large saucepan and bring to a rolling boil. Reduce the heat to low and simmer for 5–6 minutes. Strain into 4 large mugs or glasses. Serve hot.

Preparation time 10 minutes Total time 10 minutes Serves 4

limboo soda

juice of 6 limes
3 tablespoons caster sugar
10 mint leaves
1 litre/1¾ pints ice cold soda water
To serve
crushed ice and lime slices

This is one of the most refreshing drinks one can have on a hot summer's day. It also makes a terrific aperitif with a generous slug of vodka.

one In a small bowl, mix the lime juice, sugar and mint leaves, until the sugar has dissolved.

two Pour this mixture into a large jug or pitcher and add the cold soda water. Stir to mix well and pour into 4 tall glasses filled with crushed ice and lime slices.

Preparation time 5 minutes Cooking time 5–7 minutes Total time 10–12 minutes Serves 4

cardamom coffee

3 tablespoons strong freshly ground coffee
(South Indian, Colombian or Javan)
1 teaspoon crushed cardamom seeds
300 ml/½ pint milk
2 tablespoon caster sugar
750 ml/1¼ pints water

one Place the coffee, cardamom, milk, sugar and water in a large saucepan and bring to the boil. Simmer for 1–2 minutes then, using a very fine sieve lined with muslin, strain into a jug. Pour into glasses or mugs and serve hot.

Preparation time 5 minutes Cooking time 5–7 minutes Total time 10–12 minutes Serves 4

lemongrass tea

3–4 lemongrass stalks, finely chopped
4 teaspoons Indian tea leaves (Darjeeling or
Assam)
900 ml/1½ pints water
To serve:
milk
sugar

one Put the lemon grass and tea leaves in a large saucepan with the water and bring to the boil. Lower the heat and simmer, uncovered, for 2–3 minutes. Strain and serve hot, adding milk and sugar to taste.

index

index